Praise for Angie Mattson Stegall's

"The story of the journey on the Grand Canyon is inspiring and somehow also practical. It's the first time I've read a 'philosophy of life' book that comes with check lists I will use! There are wonderful ideas for consideration, yet it is not preachy. I expect to read it over and over again by checking in on a specific chapter. I thought of many people/clients who would also benefit from this book."

Christy Macchione, CCM Consulting

"This book explores *The Make Some Room Manifesto*, encouraging us to slow down and nurture ourselves. She explores the truths she learned after a 16 day rafting trip down the Colorado River through the Grand Canyon. The truths that we often don't want to face about how our lifestyle is suffocating our authentic self. Angie provides concrete, actionable steps for making space for being ALIVE, for living *your* dreams. I invite you to take Angie's dare to Make Some Room for what matters to you!"

Marsha Cayton, SEE Alternatives, LLC

"In this book, Angie uses her personal experience on a 16-day rafting trip through the Grand Canyon to illustrate some lessons that she has learned about what is important in life, and how these lessons can benefit others. She encourages readers to "make some room" — in their schedules, physical spaces, and minds — by making thoughtful and deliberate choices about how to spend their time, energy, and money. Some of her suggestions include things like using the word "no" more often and the word "busy" less often (or never!), making time for play and rest, and creating and committing to routines for dealing with potentially overwhelming amounts of "stuff" – both physical and digital." Jenni Miehle, WordDesign

---

"This book is filled with common sense ideas that we all just get too overwhelmed to think about. While relating the ideas in the book to her Grand Canyon experience, Angie takes you back to the basics and helps you see the importance of being organized, taking time for yourself and being brave. Then, when you feel that you have achieved some of those challenges, she takes you a bit deeper. Are you really connecting with people on a personal level or do you let technology get in the way? Do you take time to enjoy nature or just to breathe quietly? This is a simple, easy read filled with ideas that we all need to think about on a regular basis so we can truly enjoy life to the fullest. Reading this book will truly be worth your time, and if you follow even a few of the ideas, you will continue to reap the rewards of the time spent to read it."

Ashley Feit, Raleigh, NC

Other Books Written by
Angie Mattson Stegall

How Your Disorganization is Stealing Your Time, Your Attention and Your Health

Focus on Five: How to Organize Your Five Essential Business Systems ™

Ponder This: How Everyday Experiences Deliver Unexpected Insights in Business and Life

All books are available in Kindle format and in paperback from Amazon.com.

Sue —
I hope you enjoy reading about my adventures in making some room!

Angie Mattson Stegall

"They both listened silently to the water, which to them was not just water, but the voice of Life, the voice of Being, the voice of perpetual Becoming."
—Hermann Hesse, Siddhartha

Author: Angie Mattson Stegall

All photographs (including cover) are courtesy of Nelson Stegall (and Jenni Miehle where specifically noted).

"Make Some Room Manifesto" visual created by Jenni Miehle of WordDesign (www.worddesignstudio.net/)

First Edition
ISBN-13: 978-0692708798 (Angie Mattson-Stegall)
ISBN-10: 0692708790

By: Angie Mattson Stegall
P.O. Box 429
Pisgah Forest, NC 28768

Make Some Room

Powerful Life Lessons Inspired By an Epic 16-day Colorado River Rafting Trip Through Grand Canyon

Angie Mattson Stegall

Table of Contents

DEDICATION

This book is dedicated to my husband Nelson Stegall. Thank you for rowing and guiding us on the Colorado River through Grand Canyon upright, alive, and with joy.

THE MAKE SOME ROOM MANIFESTO

your brain is **NOT** for remembering.

| IT IS EASIER TO KEEP UP **than to catch up.** | *two minutes now* saves hours later. |

GETTING ORGANIZED is work; **STAYING ORGANIZED** is habit.

take the time. get quiet. feel into it. immerse yourself.

be discerning about where you spend your energy (reading, doing, watching, eating).

BE BOLD. BE BRAVE. *laugh.*
TAKE ACTION. *often and*
even if you're scared shitless while doing it. *loudly.*

| Reclaim your nights and weekends. | **BUSY IS A BULLSHIT WORD.** stop saying it. choose to say something real. |
| **#UNPLUG** | *keep only the useful, beautiful, and joyful.* |

we cannot know it all, read it all, keep it all, do it all, have it all, or be it all. and that's actually a good thing.

| **KILL YOUR MICROWAVE.** **THROW OUT YOUR TV.** | *stop being a mindless consumer* (of information, products, and food). start caring where "it" comes from. |

clutter is the inability (or unwillingness) to make a decision. **DECIDE.**

| PEOPLE FIRST. technology second. | *say the thing that's the hardest to say* from a place of humility and love (you'll never be sorry). |

lay in the grass and listen to the secrets it tells you. **LOVE**
smile with the flowers. hug the trees. is all there is.

SLOW DOWN. BREATHE. MAKE SOME DAMN ROOM!

A Couple of Freebies for You!

1. FREE *Make Some Room Manifesto* Postcard

I have created a lovely full-color *Make Some Room Manifesto* postcard.

If you'd like your very own copy, simply email angie@yourorganizedguide.com with your first and last name and your full mailing address. I'll mail you a full-color postcard pronto!

2. Full-Color Grand Canyon Photo Slide Show Online

Due to the cost of printing in color, I've chosen to print the photos and Manifesto in black & white for this book.

However, both the Manifesto and the photos are worth viewing in COLOR.

You can grab a full-color copy of the Manifesto (see above), plus you can view the photos from this book and a whole bunch of others from our Grand Canyon trip.

www.YukonandBean.com/grand-canyon-slideshow

Introduction

In June of 2013, my husband Nelson and I spent sixteen days rafting 225 miles of the Colorado River through Grand Canyon. Having never done a trip like this before, I wasn't really sure what to expect.

Thankfully, the friends who invited us prepared us well:

> *Take everything you think you will need.*
> *Leave everything else behind.*

Turns out, everything I needed fit into a bag about the size of a small Golden Retriever.

During our trip, our six rafts held the rest of the gear we would need: kitchen and food, bathroom setup (aka "Groovers"), and assorted emergency gear. The motto of

Grand Canyon is "Pack it in; pack it out." And that means EVERYTHING.

So, it went that I spent sixteen days sleeping under the stars and Milky Way, keeping track of trash and crumbs (called "microtrash"), and eternally trying to keep the sand out of my contact lenses.

Here's what I learned during that trip:

- It doesn't take much to keep sixteen people happy. A filling meal three times a day plus some snacks goes a long way.
- Wearing pretty much the same clothes for days on end isn't a big deal.
- Taking a bath (in the 49 degrees-cold river) every three or four days makes being clean all the sweeter.
- Nature is all around and she is beautiful. Slowing down and paying attention is like creating the most delicious meditation + prayer milkshake.
- The rapids were big and fast and the water was cold. I was scared shitless more than a few times. There was no option but to keep going. So, I did.
- Laughter, conversation, and connecting with those sixteen people were a crucial part of each day.
- I didn't think about money on the Canyon. Except for one stop at Phantom Ranch (deep at the bottom of the Canyon) for postcards and lemonade, there was literally no place to even use money. If we "needed" anything, we traded for it. Beer for toilet paper. Beer for ice. Will swim for beer! It turned out beer was quite the bartering tool.
- "Drink more water." That was the answer for everything from general crankiness to major

headaches. During this trip, I learned I was chronically dehydrated; even today, I drink three times more water now than I drank before the trip.

Simplifying your life down to a bag and a boat showed me what was important. I fell in love with the simplicity and rhythm of each day.

The *Make Some Room Manifesto*

In a world where our modern lives tend to be chaotic, noisy, and over-scheduled, making some room can be a real challenge.

My goal is to help you take a breath. Eliminate some of the chaos. Slow down.

I found that my time on the Colorado River in Grand Canyon created the space for me to think about my life very differently. This trip set the stage for me to write my *Make Some Room Manifesto*, which I'm sharing with you in detail in this book.

I created my Manifesto—my public declaration of intentions, beliefs, and opinions—after this life-changing experience showed me what was truly important.

I champion not only understanding but also moving into ACTION. So, to help you learn how to make some room in your life or in your business, I decided to turn this into a "how to" book. This book focuses on the twenty ideas outlined in my *Make Some Room Manifesto*.

I want to help you sort through the noise of life and create some space and time for you to think about simplifying your days. In the book and through the Manifesto, I show you what is important to me in hopes that it can illuminate what might be important for you.

In simple terms: I want to guide you to **make some room**.

My wish is that everyone has the opportunity to have a Grand Canyon-like experience at least once in their lives. This book is my way of sharing my personal experience. My hope is it hits you like a ton of bricks...or a two-by-four upside your head...or that it quietly but relentlessly tickles your subconscious like a gentle feather...something, anything that can wake you up to life and inspire you to begin living your life on purpose.

I believe you will benefit from what I have learned and discovered. Your only task is to focus on what resonates with you. Leave the rest behind.

But wait, how do you do this?

In a nutshell, you must figure out what is essential for you.

What is essential? It's a sweet mix of:

- your goals and values
- what you love and desire
- how you wish to make an impact in the world
- what you need and want
- and most importantly, what makes you come alive

This process of "figuring out what is essential" doesn't have to be hard; in fact, the simpler, the better.

Once you figure out the essential stuff, you can eliminate the rest. And that's where "making some room" comes in.

Since you're reading this, I assume you're ready to think about making some room in your over-stuffed life, right?

You're in the right place!

Let me end the introduction here so we can begin a journey together to guide you to make that much needed room in your life.

One final note: Each chapter of the book contains stories about my time on the river and then goes "Beyond the Canyon" with ideas, action steps, and even checklists to help you focus on what's essential for you.

I'm also thrilled to include a chapter on the Colorado River and Grand Canyon, contributed by the fantastic organization *River Runners For Wilderness*. Their mission is to promote river resource protection through wilderness management. The final chapter highlights the challenges being faced by Grand Canyon and the Colorado River. There is MUCH to be done to protect Grand Canyon, the Colorado River, and the natural spaces and waterways in our own backyards. Learn more at *https://rrfw.org.*

Chapter 1: Your brain is not for remembering.

"Never memorize something you can look up."
—Albert Einstein

My group of sixteen brave souls floated, rowed, and paddled the emerald waters of the Colorado River through Grand Canyon for sixteen days. We covered 225 river miles (plus many more miles of hiking on side trips). We were physically exhausted at the end of most days.

Our brains were exhausted some days, too. Taxed to the max in some situations, from knowing where we were on the river at any time, to anticipating the rapids coming up, and finally from the planning involved in finding a suitable camp by day's end. Each day, our group leaders had major decisions to keep up with throughout the trip.

Thankfully, we relied on several tools to assist us so we weren't trying to "remember it all."

Our trip leaders used guidebooks to help them plan and prepare. We all used checklists to gather our gear before packing and launching. Our supply company used checklists to pack our kitchen and emergency boxes and to pack our coolers with sixteen days' worth of food. And they provided us with recipes (checklists, again) to help us prepare that food into satisfying (and, some days, morale-boosting) meals.

All of our oarsmen (rowers) and kayakers used their brains to read the water and determine the right lines to run the rapids as safely as possible. We used our brains to tie up our boats safely at each stop and keep those boats in place overnight. And our Groover team (think portable potties) used their brains creatively to pick the best spots with the most glorious views for our bathroom setup.

We all helped each other remember to "wash your hands" and "drink more water."

Tools for the trip

Our first tool for the trip was the humble checklist that helped us prepare and pack for the trip. This *"What to bring on a summer river trip"* list, provided to us by our trip leaders, was super helpful in creating piles of necessary items and checking them off as we packed our gear bags. Because there are simply ZERO resources available in the Canyon, you must be sure you have everything you need (and hope you don't pack too much that you don't).

Our second tool included a printout of the rapids with their descriptions and a couple of books with specific river miles and campsite locations. During this trip, we needed to be aware of how far apart campsites were and what size group the camp could accommodate, and we needed to be careful not to be too ambitious about running major rapids at the end of a day when everyone was already tired. It was a logistical challenge, and despite the majority of our group having one or more trips under our belts, having the books as guides was important. Things could have gone massively wrong if our trip leaders had relied solely on their memories!

In writing this book, I realized again how faulty *my* memory can be. For instance, I kept a journal throughout my Grand Canyon trip. Reading it brings back memories of things I'd forgotten, funny quotes people said, and even descriptions of some of the sunsets and night views. Plus, there's something about looking over our photographs that brings the trip back into focus. It's still magical to look at the pictures of the people, rafts, colors of the water, and the beauty of the Canyon herself.

Without that journal, my brain simply wouldn't have retained all those glorious details. I'm so glad I wrote them down. Even better, others took photos and shared them with the group as well.

Re-reading my experiences and reviewing the photos helped me reconnect with how I felt on the trip the moments I was so relaxed, the moment I realized I hadn't thought about money *at all*, and even (especially) during the moments of terror crashing through some of the bigger rapids.

Beyond the Canyon

Let's face it: your life, and brain, are getting fuller by the minute. For better or worse, technology is adding complexities and layers your grandparents never had to deal with. Heck, you're barely dealing with all the details that fill up your life, right? I mean, just think about how many passwords you have in this modern world. It's mind-boggling!

Thankfully, adhering to one simple strategy—your brain is not for remembering—will go a long way toward taking the pressure off of your overloaded noggin'.

"If my brain isn't for remembering," you think, "then what is my brain for?"

Your beautiful brain is for creating, thinking, strategizing, and taking action.

Day-to-day, you may feel you don't have room in your head (or schedule) for creating, thinking and strategizing because you're so worried about forgetting something important.

You try so hard to remember something by keeping it "on your mind" or "top of mind."

The problem is, your brain simply wasn't made for this (nor is it good at it)! This causes you anxiety. Frankly, in a world where there are so many other details competing for your attention, trying to remember everything is lunacy.

What's the solution?

Use your tools and technology—instead of your brain—to help you remember.

Tools and technology can be anything from a simple list on paper to a more sophisticated piece of software that does the "remembering" for you.

Ways to make some room:

- Create a system or process for an action or activity that is repetitive (like posting your blog to your website and sharing it through social media).
- Write a checklist for recurring activities (like packing for trips or grocery shopping).
- Set recurring appointment, holiday, or birthday reminders using your electronic/online calendar.
- Start an "auto-order" or "repeat order" through your grocery store or online at Amazon.com for purchases you make repeatedly throughout the week, month, or year.
- Use a to-do list to get things off your mind and captured in ONE place.
- Schedule your next appointment as soon as the current one is over.
- Use reminders in your calendar (instead of relying on your memory).
- Capture names, addresses (snail-mail and email), phone numbers, and other pertinent information into an address book or contact list online (instead of on sticky notes, papers, and napkins scattered throughout your life).

The idea is to remove the responsibility of "remembering" from your brain and assigning it to your tools and technology in every area of your life (and business).

It's amazing how much calmer you'll feel once you've done a "brain dump" and captured all those loose ideas, tasks, and to-dos that are currently banging around in your head.

It's also amazing how much more prepared you are for any activity when you use a checklist to get ready for it. It worked for me on the Grand Canyon, and it can work for you in your daily life.

Your brain will thank you for making this change by rewarding you with more calm and creativity and by delivering up better solutions to issues, problems, dilemmas, and more.

ACTION STEP

Think of one repetitive thing you do daily or weekly. Sit down and create a checklist for it. Be it business or personal, your brain will thank you for it!

Chapter 2: It is easier to keep up than to catch up.

Admittedly, the part of my Grand Canyon trip that I found least appealing was packing and unpacking the boats each day. The set-up and tear-down routines took time, effort, and coordination. Especially at the beginning of the trip, I struggled to carry heavy items through the sand, and sometimes up sandy hills, for them to be set up. Kitchen areas, bathroom areas, and our chosen sleeping areas required the most effort because of the sheer volume of items to load and unload.

But the more organized and cooperative we were during unloading and setup each evening, the faster we found the whole routine got done. Each morning when we packed up, the more methodical and consistent we were, the faster we were able to finish and get going down the river. I can only imagine how things might have gone if our group was sloppy about organization. Consequences could have ranged from annoying (where did we put the hand wash stations this time?) to severe (a boat flips in a rapid and stuff not tied down is lost to the river).

We also found it easier and more courteous to complete tasks all the way rather than leaving something for the next meal or the next day. Just think—if we'd left dirty dishes for the evening crew, not only would dinner be delayed but we'd also potentially open ourselves up to bacteria and illness that could have jeopardized the whole group. Plus, leaving dirty dishes is just rude—I mean, how cranky would that have made the team?

Another area where we focused on being thorough was keeping up with the trash, including the tiny particles of food and other debris called "microtrash." Although the National Park Service limits the number of trips and people allowed on the Canyon at any one time, there's still incredible pressure on the environment from those who do float the river.

Campsites are used almost daily throughout the warmer months. And with sixteen people eating and sleeping and coming and going, trash is bound to happen. One of the very last things you are required to do is scan your camping area for microtrash. If you see any bit of trash (whether it's yours or not), you pick it up. It doesn't even matter how small (think cigarette butts, dental floss, twist ties, and other bits of paper and plastic). By keeping up with the microtrash, you avoid having to organize a big clean up later on. And you protect the animals, the camping area, the water—heck, the whole Grand Canyon environment—from becoming a big trash can.

Another way we kept up was through putting things back where we found them and sticking to routines for setup, cooking, cleaning, and tear down. Keeping to these small routines helped us "keep up" with our communal and personal stuff and with each other.

Beyond the Canyon

I think my sister was the first person I ever heard say, *"It is easier to keep up than to catch up."*

I'm pretty sure it's not her original saying, yet it is good advice. And it's advice I share often now because it applies to so many different areas of our lives:

- losing weight
- getting organized
- using technology
- doing the dishes
- taking out the garbage
- sleeping
- working
- exercising
- traveling
- starting anything
- quitting anything

I also love *"it is easier to keep up than catch up"* because it asks me to focus on the essentials. I can't keep up with everything—I simply don't have enough time, energy, or attention. If I keep running out of time, or energy, or attention, I'll be always trying to catch up. See how this works?

Rather, when I focus on the essentials, when I focus on doing less, I know I'll be able to more effectively keep up— and quit playing that losing game of "catch up."

Let me share a more common, real-world example that you might be able to relate to:

You get mail, right? And a bunch of it, I'd bet. See if any of the follow scenarios ring a bell for you:

Scenario #1—The Avoider: You go out to the mailbox and see a big stack. You shut the box and walk away.

"Too overwhelming," you think.

Scenario #2—The Pile Maker: You pull the big stack of mail out of the mailbox, walk into the kitchen, and drop it on the counter.

"I'll get to it later," you sigh. And off you go to the next thing on your mind.

Scenario #3—The Distracted One: You take the big stack of mail and flip through it. Some is obviously junk mail, so you chuck it in the trash. A few things need action and you stick them back on the counter. Some stuff might need to be shredded. You create another pile and think, "I'm hungry. What's for dinner?" as you head to the fridge.

Scenario #4—The One Who Gets It Done: In just under two minutes, you retrieve the mail from the mailbox and walk inside to your desk. You plow through the pile with determination and focus. Bills to be paid go on the desk in the same spot every time. Junk mail goes in the trash. Unwanted papers and circulars go in the recycle bin. The shredder is right next to the trash, so you shred the few information-sensitive pages. You make a note about something and put it with the bills. Magazines to be read go on the table by the reading lamp. Done. No new piles are created because everything has a place to go.

Which example sounds like you?

Which example do you wish was you?

Keeping Up

It's easier to keep up with recurring events (like the mail, which—in the United States anyway—comes six out of seven days, rain or shine) than to try catch up when the stack is three feet tall and feels overwhelming.

The same argument can be made for email, filing papers, returning phone calls, returning something "back to its place," or even flossing your teeth (as an aside—my friend Beverly says you only have to floss the ones you want to keep).

So, how can YOU keep up?

Ways to make some room

I say learn to adopt and love routines!

Go back and read #4 in the mail scenario above. One routine is to become the *One Who Gets It Done.*

Create a routine for anything. Here are the steps:

1. Decide what needs to be done.
2. Commit to it (daily, weekly, monthly, yearly).
3. Gather the supplies you need (if any).
4. Carve out and dedicate the time (even if it's two minutes once a day).
5. Do the thing.
6. Give yourself a Big High-Five!

Whether you're in a sensitive eco-system like Grand Canyon or a familiar place like your home or office, believe me when I tell you keeping up is so much easier (and efficiently effective) than catching up. Use the steps above to establish your routine. Even if you miss a day, it's so much easier to get back to the habit and keep up with it.

I will say, when we returned from our Grand Canyon trip, we had quite a huge pile of mail (and quite a backlog of email). And that's perfectly normal whenever you have a disruption in your normal routine. The key to getting back into your routine is catching up by handling the backlog as efficiently and effectively as you can. Schedule time to dig in and clear out the backlog. Be ruthless about tossing, recycling, and shredding. With email, be "delete-key-happy" and just give yourself permission to not read anything that isn't an "actionable item."

We get a lot of information pushed at us these days. Most of it is just an opportunity to help us part with our money. Resist the temptation to "take a peek" so you can more quickly get back to what's truly important.

ACTION STEP

Create a routine for anything:

1. Decide what needs to be done.
2. Commit to it (daily, weekly, monthly, yearly).
3. Gather the supplies you need (if any).
4. Carve out and dedicate the time (even if it is just two minutes once a day).
5. Do the thing.
6. Then give yourself a Big High-Five!

Chapter 3: Two minutes now saves hours later.

A no-brainer on the Canyon is to spend two minutes checking ropes and tie-downs before running any rapids. There are horror stories of tie-downs that weren't checked. The raft flips in a rapid and the entire contents of, say, a kitchen box are lost to the river. On a long trip, not having utensils, pots, and plates can be a lesson in creativity, or, at worst, a lift-threatening event.

We were fortunate that we didn't lose any gear on our trip. We were also fortunate not to lose any boats. During a different river trip over the summer, we heard about another Grand Canyon trip that had a boat get loose in the night and slip away. It was days before they found it. Perhaps if someone had taken two minutes before going to bed that night to check the ropes, the boat wouldn't have wandered away. Maybe, maybe not (because the River, she is a fickle lady). Still, with the enormous consequences of losing a boat (even temporarily), taking those two minutes seemed prudent.

I will confess something that two minutes might have saved us: a boatload of spaghetti and meatballs.

Our kitchen setup consisted of three metal tables with legs that folded in for storage and folded out for setup. We set the tables into a "U" shape for food preparation, cooking, and serving.

One day we arrived in camp and, as usual, everyone helped unload boats. On this day, the group decided to put the kitchen area up on a rise because of the great view of the river. We set up the tables, placed the stove on one of the tables, and put out other items according to their use (think utensils, pots, and plates). Then everyone scattered to unload their personal gear, set up their beds, and take care of personal needs. I may or may not have collapsed from exhaustion and the heat. Thank goodness for nap time!

As evening approached, the kitchen crew gathered what they needed to make appetizers for the group and to start cooking dinner. They pulled out a huge stockpot and filled it with water. Boiling commenced and spaghetti noodles were cooked. The kitchen crew drained off the water and added sauce and frozen meatballs to the cooked spaghetti.

Then disaster struck. Someone was stirring the giant pot of spaghetti, sauce, and meatballs. As they pulled the giant pot closer to the edge for a better stirring angle, the sand under the table shifted. The table lurched forward. The stove, pot, and table hit the sand, and the contents splattered people nearby. In addition to the disaster of splattering people with hot spaghetti sauce and flying meatballs, we had lost our DINNER.

Thankfully, no one was hurt and most of what was ruined in the sand was the bunch of meatballs still frozen on top of the sauce.

As soon as it was determined that no one got hurt, the group assembled quickly for a discussion. If the setup folks had taken two minutes to properly "set" the tables deeply in the sand, the collapsing table incident might not have happened. All around, everyone agreed to slow down, double check what we were doing, and ensure the safety of the group at all times. That, and we started strapping the table legs together in that "U" shape (you know, just to be safe).

Beyond the Canyon

Two minutes now saves hours later.

This idea is about **saving time** versus spending time.

After all, who doesn't like to save? And who among us isn't feeling time-starved?

Part of the beauty of keeping up is in understanding how spending two minutes now can literally save you hours later.

Let's keep going with the mail example from chapter two, shall we?

Suppose you identify with Scenarios #1 (The Avoider) or #2 (The Piler) or #3 (The Distracted One).

Let me explain very simply how failing to take two minutes now can turn into hours of trouble, tracking, and handling later.

Here's the scene: you come home, grab mail from the box, and sling in onto the kitchen counter as you walk in the door. Each day you repeat this until you have a stack that's nearly three feet tall.

In aggravation, you quickly sift through the pile and pick out bills, personal notes, and other readily identifiable pieces. The rest, you sweep into the recycle bin. Recycling is good right?

Unbeknownst to you, there's a person who arrives at 4:30 a.m. each day with a small flashlight. He sorts through those recycling bins looking for personal mail and, especially, credit card offers. He finds a few of yours and—presto—opens a couple new accounts in your name. Can you say "identity theft?"

Now, you only realize this identity theft has happened when (a) you get a bill in the mail (assuming you open it), (b) you check your credit report once a year, and/or (c) your fraud protection through your bank kicks in and they call about suspicious activity.

Regardless of how you find out, you still have a big mess to sort out, right?

Just think, if you had taken two minutes each day to sort the mail and shred the sensitive stuff, you wouldn't be the victim of identity theft!

And let's not mention late fees that happen when you don't open your mail in a timely manner. Or the amount of time it will take you to sort out the issue.

It's similar to strapping the tables together to ensure that no spaghetti, sauce, or meatballs are harmed at dinnertime. Similar, but kinda different.

Are you getting my drift here?

Taking two minutes to handle something now saves hours of problems, aggravation, searching and cleaning up later.

Ways to make some room

In the real world, people still get burned by flying spaghetti sauce (literally or proverbially). That being said, there are a ton of more practical ways for you to keep up instead of having to catch up.

Ideally, you'll begin to discover for yourself where those two minutes of magic can make a big difference in your life.

Two minutes of attention. It ain't much...but I promise those two minutes have the power to save you hours of effort later.

Action Step

Jump on those two-minute wins! Here are some examples to get you started:

- Put your phone, wallet, and keys in the same place every day.
- Prep first (then cook).
- File, shred, trash.
- Exercise and stretch.
- Return a hard call or email instead of avoiding it.
- Say the thing that's hard to say.
- Brush and floss.
- Breathe purposefully.
- Refill your subscription or prescription before you are out.
- Go ahead and buy the big pack of toilet paper.
- Double check the tie-downs on the kayaks on top of your car (just sayin').
- Keep up with your continuing education, expiration dates on your web hosting, and more.

Chapter 4: Getting organized is work.
Staying organized is habit.

On any epic trip, but especially on Grand Canyon trips, there's so much to plan! There's organizing all of that stuff and the people using it:

- gear (backpacks, sleeping gear, boats, etc.)
- food
- emergency equipment

- people (and in some cases oarsmen and oars women)
- where to stop for lunch and where the group sleeps
- where the dangers might be (tricky places on the trail; major rapids on a river)
- plans to be shared in case something goes wrong and/or part of the team doesn't return when they say they will

Pulling together a private Grand Canyon trip is an epic production. On the morning we were to head to the put-in, sixteen of us assembled with our personal gear and bags of beer in the parking lot of a hotel.

Scene: an enormous flatbed trailer pulled by a big truck.

We'd hired an outfitter to assemble all that necessary gear and food for us. They helped us with menus and planning and cooler organization.

When they arrived with their flatbed truck, it was time to load all our personal gear up and head for the river.

On that trailer were five rafts, oars and oar rigs, waterproof boxes (called ammo cans), and several enormous coolers filled with ice and food to feed sixteen people for sixteen days.

Bags, colorful collapsible camp chairs, kayaks, helmets, paddles, life vests, beverages, and more littered the parking lot. Eventually, everything was loaded and tied securely for the several-hour drive to the Lee's Ferry put-in.

When we arrived at the put-in, everyone piled out of the vans and we formed a production line. The rafts were laid out and inflated. Oar rigs were assembled and strapped to the boats. Then we walked the boats down to the water's edge so we could load and strap down coolers and gear boxes. Our supply company handed out oars and rafts were assigned to oarsmen and passengers (like me). Finally, we stocked the ammo boxes, personal gear bags, and assorted odds and ends into the boats and made sure everything was strapped down securely. It took several hours in the very, very hot sunshine and 110 degree heat. We drank gallons of water, used tons of sunscreen, and wore hats.

At the put-in, Grand Canyon Park Rangers inspected our life vests, checked our launch paperwork, and identification. Then the ranger gave a lighthearted but serious talk about the cold water (49 degrees at the put-in), the heat (we were expecting highs nearing 115 during the day), and the animals, reptiles, and bugs of the Canyon. We discussed emergency plans and confirmed we carried a satellite phone.

From the very beginning of the trip, organization and teamwork were *strongly encouraged.* The safety of the group depended on us adopting a routine day-in and day-out and sticking to it. From unloading and reloading the boats to washing our hands before each meal and every time we used the bathroom, staying organized and developing habits were KING.

It took us a couple days to settle into those habits and routines, and with just a few issues (see the spaghetti story in the last chapter), those organizational habits held us in good stead.

As an example, with limited space, the kitchen boxes needed to be repacked carefully. The whole of the kitchen boat did as well. Our teams were most successful when one person (the main oarsman or woman) handled the packing and organization for each boat. And each individual did well to keep their own personal gear organized. Losing gear on a long trip is no fun. By putting items back in a methodical, thoughtful way, we ensured everything was there—and noticed right away when something was missing.

I believe there are no small numbers of sandals left behind at campsites throughout Grand Canyon (and probably all over the world).

From the beginning, we tried to organize our kitchen duties and the schedule. We organized how we loaded and unloaded boats. Our Groover team organized itself into an efficient potty set-up and tear-down machine.

Beyond the Canyon

I think now is a good time to reveal a couple of life's truths that I saw in action during our trip and that I've seen in real life:

> *Getting organized is WORK.*
> *Staying organized is habit.*

In the larger scheme of life, I realize how just a few key habits will go a long way toward keeping me (and my team or family) organized.

First, though, I want to go on a tiny rant. It is something that I feel really strongly about, and I hope you will hear me out.

There are no magic bullets when it comes to getting organized.

There just aren't. I become really frustrated when people expect the process of getting organized to be fast and easy. (In contrast, the process of *staying organized* can be quite fast and easy.)

I've discovered that getting organized isn't fast and easy usually because most people have TOO MUCH and they are reluctant to let things go. Examples of "too much" can include:

- schedules
- closets
- kitchen drawers and cabinets
- brains
- file drawers
- travel bags and suitcases
- backpacks
- itineraries
- goals
- bookshelves
- more

It is my personal rant to say: you are spending too much time on unimportant things like email, TV, and internet surfing. Your to-do lists are too long. Your "to-read" piles are too high. You have too many bookmarks on the computer. And you try to squish too many obligations into any time you can find.

It really is all TOO MUCH.

I do not know how I, you, or we can keep up this pace. I see it on the faces of business people, moms, dads, and every-day, average people I talk to. Everybody is overwhelmed, and it is coming to a point in our society where it's nearly unmanageable. We are becoming fat, sick, and broke (there's even a movie out with the same name).

My answer to this sickness of too much? It's really simple:

Stop doing so much. Stop having so much. And even stop *thinking* so much.

Seriously, give yourself permission to step away from the "too much."

#endrant

Let's talk commitment

When I think about getting organized and maintaining that organization as a habit, I think of one thing:

COMMITMENT.

When I decided to participate in this Grand Canyon experience, I basically committed on Day 1 (the day we pushed away from shore). Between the put-in there at Lee's Ferry and the takeout sixteen days later, there were only two ways I could leave: at Phantom Ranch on day seven or eight (which then requires a seven-plus mile hike out) or by helicopter (but only if I was *seriously* injured). Otherwise, I was committed to floating the entire 225 miles over sixteen days.

I've found the same is true (though the consequences are usually not so severe) for me to say YES to a commitment to getting and staying organized.

A commitment starts with a decision. Decide what I want. Decide how I think I'll get it. Then commit myself to the actions needed to reach my goal.

For the longest time, I couldn't even spell commitment, much less really understand what it meant. A gifted coach cleared things up for me. "It's about integrity, Angie," she said. "You figure out what you want, commit to it, make a plan, and follow through."

Everywhere in this book, I'd like you to think long and hard about any changes you get excited about making. Choose small steps and manageable goals. Commit to them. And with integrity, follow through. In the beginning, it might feel like work. With commitment and practice comes the ease of habit.

Getting and staying organized

Being on this sixteen-day river trip allowed me to simplify. To slow down. To make room for my thoughts, for my friends, and for the sheer pleasure of doing nothing but staring at the river.

On this trip, I realized exactly how little it takes for me personally to be blissfully happy.

I realized exactly how little the group and I needed to "do" to be comfortable and content.

It's a lesson that applies off the river, too.

In fact, realizing how little we used and needed kick-started an effort by my husband Nelson and me to really purge our stuff. Now, we live in about 280 square feet and love only having the stuff we need.

I want to encourage YOU to try it! Use the first few chapters as your blueprint:

- Keep up rather than catch up.
- Two minutes now saves hours later.
- Staying organized trumps getting organized every time.

BONUS CHALLENGE: box up everything you own. For one solid month, only go into the boxes for things you need. Keep them out only if you use them regularly. Give the things you keep out and use regularly a specific "place" in your home. Everything left in those boxes? They have the potential to be sold, donated, or given away.

Ways to make some room

Every single day in the Canyon had a routine. Each meal had a menu, and each day had assigned kitchen leaders. Trip leaders made decisions based on weather, miles, and where we would camp each night. Boat captains packed and unpacked their boats the same way each day.

Routines were critical for ensuring everything went back in the boat where it belonged, no straps were left loose, and all people and their belongings were in the rafts ready to go each morning. Safety was key, and the key to safety was people paying attention to their routines.

Routines become guidelines—lines of guidance—to help you anchor your day, your activities, and even your attitude.

Just a few simple routines support you staying organized and become the foundation for a successful and fulfilling life.

A final note: your thoughts, habits, and choices today determine who you are tomorrow. Be purposeful and deliberate and choose them wisely.

(See your Action Step on the next page.)

ACTION STEP

Here are two examples of daily routines you could adopt. Adapt them for yourself.

Morning
- meditation
- exercise/yoga
- sitting still while enjoying a cup of coffee or tea
- writing or journaling
- preparing for the day and week

Evening
- tidying your office before you leave
- creating a to-do list for your next day
- meditation
- exercise
- savoring a meal with friends or family
- taking a hot bath
- writing or journaling

SIMPLICITY is KEY

Chapter 5: Take the time, get quiet, feel into it. Immerse yourself.

Grand Canyon is a harsh place, full of extremes, but it is also a place of profound beauty.

Part of the magic of such an immersive trip as the Grand Canyon is the opportunity to get off the water and explore the Canyon by foot. There are tons of things to see, do, discover, and explore in between the miles on the river, in between the towering walls.

And being where we were, in a remote place, with little chance of getting help if we needed it, we had to pay attention even as we were exploring. During our hikes, we stayed aware of where we placed our feet, and we watched where we put our hands. Things in the Canyon are sharp, pointy, hot, and hard...and some of them sting and bite.

Throughout our trip, the waters of the Colorado River remained a brilliant emerald green. Views during side hikes were breathtaking. One memorable side hike in particular led us up and up and up to a place called "The Patio" at Deer Creek. The hike up was long and hot; switchbacks allowed us to catch glimpses of the glimmering river below.

At the top of this hike, we carefully traversed a very narrow ledge trail next to a narrow slot canyon. From this ledge, I could see a clear downward view of a narrow slot canyon. Through this narrow sluice, and rushing to its end, the water poured over the side as a huge, roaring waterfall.

Reaching the end of the narrow ledge trail, the area opened up and we got our reward: up here, the rock slabs were flat and wide, and the creek was shallow, clear, and cold. Greenery and trees grew in the shade, nourished by the reliable water source.

Here, all my senses were involved. I moved away from the other people to better enjoy the quiet. Compared to the heat at the bottom of the Canyon, this cool, green, shaded patio-like area was a delicious reward. I was beyond grateful for the break from the steep climb and from the relentless heat. Up here, I could smell the dampness in the air. I crushed some greenery between my fingers and gave it a good sniff. Standing in the middle of the creek, I splashed cold water on my face, feeling invigorated, marveling at how beautiful and surprising this area turned out to be.

After an easier and speedier hike down, my group climbed back aboard our rafts feeling rejuvenated and happy for the experience. We felt calmer and completely immersed in nature. All of our senses were enlivened.

Many of the side hikes on this trip were a mixture of awe-inducing views and laughter-inducing fun. We each took time to get quiet and feel into the experiences; we were "all in," and these experiences changed us for the better.

Beyond the Canyon

The whole premise of my *Make Some Room Manifesto* (see page 9 to view the full Manifesto) is to remind myself to take time and make some room in my life. This affects everything I do, have, and even how I "*be.*"

As I slow down, take time, get quiet, and begin to feel again, life changes. I change.

Arianna Huffington, in her book *Thrive*, shares four reasons to let your mind wander:

- You use a different kind of intellect.
- It enhances your ability to think creatively.
- You become more empathetic.
- It's a portal to self-discovery.

Sometimes the answers come when you slow down, give yourself time to feel your way into a problem, and immerse your whole self in it.

"How do I do that?" you might be asking.

Easy: sit and do nothing.

Gratefully, this requires you to buy nothing and have no special skills and really asks for no commitment beyond your agreement to actually sit there.

Begin slowly!

- Try small amounts of time (five or ten minutes).
- Find a comfortable place.
- Choose to look at something that makes you feel peaceful (for example, a photo of your pet or child, a flower, or a candle/flame). Really notice the feeling of peace.
- Prepare NOT to be interrupted for however long you choose—turn off your electronic devices, inform the people in your life you wish to be undisturbed (this is an excellent exercise in setting and holding self-care boundaries).
- Pay attention to your breath—this helps you focus, center, and be calm.
- Relax! Don't worry about a certain way to sit or about perfect posture. Choose to be comfortable.
- **Practice:** starting at your toes, tense-up your muscles (one at a time) and relax them, moving up your body tensing and relaxing your muscles all the way to the top of your head. This does take some focus and some practice. Give it a try! You'll feel decidedly different by the end of the exercise.
- Continue to practice "doing nothing" daily (but maybe not *all day*).

In the weirdest, most wonderful way, doing nothing actually helps me feel into life; I become immersed in it!

And this doing nothing is one of my favorite "something" to-do activities.

A bit more challenging—engage in full-on PLAY!

Researcher, storyteller, and author Brené Brown has done a ton of research on play. She's found that making time to play can actually benefit our work. During play we find joy, satisfaction, and even excitement. When we engage in "true play" we find it benefits our work in ways we never expected. Soon, play becomes crucial for us to maintain satisfying, long-term work.

In a nutshell: LIFE does not WORK without PLAY.

Go and do whatever it is that makes you smile, feel like a kid, connects you with your spirit, gets your hands dirty, covers you with paint and glitter, and makes your stomach hurt from laughing.

Ways to make some room

Play and/or full immersion in an activity:

- painting
- drawing
- building structures (blanket caves, box forts, stick shelters)
- make believe using anything in nature
- sports
- pottery
- jewelry making
- sketching
- singing

- role playing wearing costumes
- creating rhymes or poems
- dancing
- make believe using action figures or other toys
- chasing, tagging, tumbling, running
- cooking
- work (yes, you can get fully immersed in work)
- your ideas...

Martha Beck (the well-known life coach and author of many best-selling books) has banished the word "work" from her vocabulary. Now, she playfully invites you to "play until it's time to rest and rest until it is time to play."

(See your Action Step on the next page.)

ACTION STEP

Rest, Play, Be Wild

Go and do whatever it is that makes you smile, feel like a kid, connects you with your spirit, gets your hands dirty, covers you with paint and glitter, and makes your stomach hurt from laughing.

This could be anything from sitting quietly watching the birds and chipmunks do their thing to dancing naked in the backyard while running through the sprinklers.

It's completely your choice. Do what makes you HAPPY.

Running the "rapids" on the Little Colorado River,
photo courtesy of Jenni Miehle

Chapter 6: Be discerning about where you spend your energy (reading, doing, watching, eating).

My husband Nelson and I are both self-employed. When our friends approached us in January of 2013 to ask us if we wanted to claim two seats on a sixteen-day, 225-mile Grand Canyon trip, we said YES almost without thinking about it.

Rafting the Colorado River through Grand Canyon has been something Nelson has wanted to do since he was a boy. After college, he was a raft guide on the New River in West Virginia. It was a "bucket list" thing for him to be an oarsman and run the Grand Canyon. This trip would be a personal challenge for me, since I get weak-kneed just thinking about running big rapids.

Nelson and I knew we'd have to coordinate care for our pets, save money since we wouldn't be working for almost a month, and let our clients know we'd be unavailable during that time. Somehow, everything came together perfectly and the trip was one we will never forget.

Taking the time to just be on this trip did wonders for us. Those sixteen days went fast and were full of daily routines and activities. But the trip did allow us time for thinking, doing nothing, and talking about life.

When we returned, both of us started being more discerning about the clients we worked with. We rented out our house in a town we didn't love living in and moved to the mountains. We got married. And life is so much better for having made those changes.

Beyond the Canyon

So, the title of chapter is "Be discerning about where your energy." Let's dive into this *discernment* thing, shall we? After all, discernment is one of one of my favorite words.

The definition of discerning is: *being able to see and understand people, things, or situations clearly.*

Discerning is about choosing. It's not "remembering." It's being present in the moment, making a judgment call, and choosing the best available option *for you*.

Being discerning is a huge part of making some room because being able to see and understand clearly often requires you step back, take stock, and make a deliberately considered choice.

Being discerning about where I spend my energy is a biggie for me. I mean, I have basically unlimited choice.

When I go to the grocery store, I see an unending amount of food (or food-like substances) to choose from.

Television? How about 1,000 channels (and perhaps still nothing to watch)?

Reading? Amazon.com currently has millions of books available. And I can pick up a book in my hands, or read it on a device, or listen to it. I have SO many options!

In a world that feels too full (at least to me), one of the smartest actions I can take is to NOT drink from the fire hose that is life.

When I think of a fire hose, I think of something that takes several firefighters to control. The torrent of water shooting out of the hose is unbelievable. And it takes a team to turn the water on and off. The power of that fire hose is immense...too much for one person to handle.

Instead, I imagine my options as a common garden hose. When I turn on a garden hose, I see a small stream, much more manageable. I can control it with ease and turn it on or off at will with the twist of the spigot.

For me, this image means I am responsible for what information I allow to be PUSHED at me. By limiting what I allow into my frame of reference (email, snail mail box, grocery cart, and even my home), I can more successfully turn down the pressure to a more manageable flow.

When I think about limiting what I allow to be pushed at me, I include all *six* of my senses:

1. sight
2. sound
3. taste
4. touch
5. smell
6. feeling (internal—different from touch)

I choose to slow down. I stop saying "yes" to everything. I take time to think about what I'm doing and why I'm doing it. Rather than trying to squish it all in and figure out how to do more, more, more better, I consider what might happen if I instead focused simply on doing less, well.

When I feel overwhelmed, I ask myself: what can I stop doing? I take a very conscious look at what I'm trying to jam into my schedule. I reconsider all the emails in my inbox and use the delete key with glee. I throw away and recycle papers and magazines. I cancel appointments. I drink more water. I take naps.

Gentle reader, consider how you can turn off the fire hose.

Yes, right now.

Take a few deep breaths. Check in with yourself. Keep breathing until the crazy-person feeling subsides.

Instead, ask yourself:

- What matters to me?
- What are my priorities?

- Who are my priorities?
- Am I acting and living my priorities?

And then ask, "Am I embodying, creating, manifesting, and/or leading my life with these priorities?

It is really important that you are very clear on what you want and what is good for you, what feeds you, what you give your attention to.

Think of it this way: what is your true heart's desire? How can you create that in your life?

Remember, nothing will change until you decide to change it. The power and choice are yours.

- If you're tired of feeling overwhelmed, stop. Figure out how not to be overwhelmed.
- If your life is chaotic, stop (even for just a few minutes). Figure out how to not be chaotic.
- And if you're stressed out, by all means, stop for an hour or two. Take some deep breaths. Figure out how to eliminate what (or whom) is causing your stress.

Ways to make some room—by acting with discernment

In order to begin acting with discernment, it's important to simply stop and pay attention to what is causing your overwhelm. Once you've pinpointed the problem area(s), you can move on to solutions:

- I will not live like this anymore.
- I am not working like this anymore.

- This relationship is not working anymore.
- These clothes aren't working anymore.
- This house/neighborhood/city isn't working for me anymore.
- Enough is enough.
- Fill in the blank: I'm done with_____.

Sometimes the easiest place to start is by paraphrasing the hilarious writer, Anne Lamott. She simply says a complete sentence is two letters: NO.

The most beneficial practice I have learned is to say "No," or at least, "Not right now." Other graceful language includes, "I'll get back to you on this. I want some time to consider this. Let me sit with it for twenty-four hours and I'll be back in touch with my answer."

If it isn't a clear YES, it's a NO.

- No.
- No, not now.
- No, not today.
- No, never.
- No, thank you.

Using the word NO powerfully, strategically, deliberately, purposefully—this will revolutionize your life! It's also the epitome of being discerning.

And do not apologize for your NO. Said succinctly, and with grace, a NO said with conviction is all the explanation needed.

Self-Awareness—when to say NO

- tension between what you feel is right (in your gut) and what someone is pressuring you to do
- conflict between internal conviction and external action
- saying YES when you mean NO but still doing it only to avoid conflict or friction
- feeling too scared to turn down a request from colleague, boss, friend, neighbor, etc. because they "might" be disappointed or angry

Try five seconds of discomfort now instead of five days/weeks/months of resentment later.

Finally, go for long-term respect over short-term popularity.

If you cannot say no or if you cannot let go of something, consider that there may be a little bit of inner work you must do first. There are reasons you're resistant to letting go of a toxic relationship; reasons you cannot seem to ever get organized; even reasons why you've decided it is okay for you to hate your schedule and still keep up the breakneck pace anyway.

Once you can do the inner work, you can allow yourself the option of choosing something different, more fulfilling, and perhaps even—gasp!—something more FUN!

Making the choice to do less can be magical. This is you paying attention to how you are using your time and choosing something bigger, better, different...or choosing to do nothing at all (this is called RESTING, by the way).

And after you rest, you are more able to be discerning, to say NO to what doesn't serve you, and to have the energy to say YES to those things that are in alignment with your desires and priorities.

Ways to make some room

When you find yourself overwhelmed, overworked, and neglecting your self-care, here are some thoughts to ponder:

- Am I doing what I am doing out of fear (of being alone or misunderstood, failing, or feeling unloved)?
- Am I feeling unworthy?
- Am I afraid they won't like me if I say no?
- Am I taking this client because I desperately need the money?
- Am I afraid if I say no, I will never have this (opportunity/chance/thing) again?
- Am I doing it out of a need for security, approval, or certainty?
- Do I need to keep these belongings because I might need them at some point later?
- If I give these away, will the people who gave (or gifted) them to me not like me anymore?
- Should I keep this just in case I might need it later? If I give the thing away and the person finds out, will it upset them and/or hurt their feelings?
- Maybe I should keep it for an emergency?
- Will I need it later?
- If I've always had it, should I keep it?

- If I've always done it this way, shouldn't I keep doing it this way?

Gentle reader, believe me when I say the act of being discerning (choosing wisely and exercising the power of NO) actually helps you make some room. And in making room, you find energy, attention, answers, creativity, and more.

ACTION STEP

Answer these questions and you'll be much farther along the path of satisfaction and happiness. You'll avoid procrastination. And you'll end your overwhelm.

1. What IS the best and highest use of my time?
2. What are my God-given gifts and talents?
3. What do I love doing?
4. What can I STOP doing?

Chapter 7: Be bold. Be brave. Take action. (Even if you're scared shitless while doing it.)

I always joke that I was designed for comfort, not for speed. Whitewater especially terrifies me because of the speed at which things happen.

A few years ago, I decided to try whitewater kayaking since so many of friends seemed to prefer that to the mellower version of lakes and slow, meandering rivers that I preferred (known as sea kayaking or touring kayaking).

I gave whitewater kayaking a real try: bought my own boat, helmet, paddle, and PFD (personal flotation device), all specialty gear designed for whitewater. I went to practice to learn how to roll my boat at the local pool. I paid for lessons to learn to read the water and run rapids with a great female kayak instructor. And I did it. I ran rapids. Had a great on-side roll. And I did okay running actual rivers. Except I was scared shitless almost the entire time, every time, I was in my boat.

I finally realized it was not fun for me.

So I quit.

Thus, when the call came to raft the Grand Canyon, it was a terrified YES that came out of my mouth.

I was terrified during our first big rapids. I was terrified in the mornings as we re-packed our boats and everyone talked in sometimes-hushed tones about the day's BIG rapids. I cried as we squared up to enter those BIG rapids.

One passage from the journal I kept during my trip through the Canyon summed up my fears:

> *"I'm scared! Scared of scorpions, snakes, rapids, and group dynamics. I also really see I have control issues. Being a passenger on an eighteen-foot inflatable rubber raft being rowed by my beloved (who hasn't rowed a raft in nearly twenty years) does not lend itself to feeling 'in control.'"*

And then something remarkable happened. Just before one enormous, roaring rapid, Nelson came back after scouting it, his face looking pale and pinched. All he said to me was, "Don't fall out of the boat." I saw on his face how truly scared he was this time. My journal notes continued:

"I started to cry quietly as we approached the first set of big rapids. The terror and the tears continued even as Nelson successfully navigated us—upright and alive—through them. At some point in the trip, in order to stop focusing on the terror, I started counting. Running most big rapids took all of fourteen seconds."

Fourteen seconds of fear. That was it.

Fourteen seconds of being scared shitless but doing it anyway.

And just like that, my fears became smaller, more manageable. I realized fourteen seconds goes by in a flash, even though when I'm in a rapid, time slows down considerably, to the point that splashes of water happen in slow motion, as the boat rises and dips like a big blue swan, in and out of the churning waves.

Fourteen seconds was long enough for Nelson to lose an oar and holler at me for help and for me to reach into the roiling waters to retrieve it. We made it through that rapid upright and successfully, too.

Thus, I learned how to be bold and brave in fourteen-second intervals.

And I believe you can, too.

Beyond the Canyon

I want to begin with something called the "Hero's Journey." A mythologist named Joseph Campbell first identified the Hero's Journey back in 1949. There are typically four parts.

1. The Call
2. Refusal of the Call
3. The Journey
4. The Return

The Hero's Journey matters because sooner or later, each of us will be called to one (if we're paying attention).

The Hero must accept the call and step into the Journey of adventure. The Journey is full of obstacles and tests the Hero must overcome. It's hard, grueling, and at times feels impossible.

Making it through the Journey is the reward. For after the Journey, the Hero can look back and see the lessons, feel the strength he or she has gained, and have the opportunity to take this newfound knowledge out into the world.

The Grand Canyon trip was a big "calling" for me. Would I accept this Call to the adventure? A big part of me wanted to refuse. I was scared. Not sure I could do it.

But I accepted the Call, nerves and doubts and all. I went on the trip. It wasn't easy. At the beginning of the trip, I didn't take care of myself and suffered from swelling in my legs and migraines—all because I didn't drink enough water. I was exhausted through parts of the trip from the relentless schedule of packing and unpacking our gear. I got sick of the sand and the heat. I cried at times in fear and frustration. I even had doubts about Nelson's skills when we got to first few really big rapids.

In the end, though, this small Journey was a Big Calling for me and for Nelson. It gave us a new perspective on life. It re-invigorated us. And it helped us change everything for the better.

Examples of Hero's Journeys in pop culture

Did you know some of the most successful movies ever made have a Hero's Journey as a big part of their plot lines?

- Mark Hamill as Luke Skywalker in *Star Wars*
- Jennifer Lawrence as Katniss Everdeen in *Hunger Games*
- Tom Hanks as Captain Phillips in *Captain Phillips*
- Mel Gibson as William Wallace in *Braveheart*
- Daniel Day Lewis as Nathaniel Poe in *Last of the Mohicans*
- All of the stories written by J.R.R. Tolkien
- *Chronicles of Narnia* book by C.S. Lewis
- *Avatar* by James Cameron
- Many children's fairy tales/stories

I'm deeply inspired by people who answered the Call by following their dreams or by making a difference in the real world. I find them to be bold and brave, using their unique voices, and living life in their own special ways.

Here are some examples of my heroes:

Danielle LaPorte, author of _The Fire Starter Sessions_ and creator of _The Desire Map_, is a strong example of someone doing life her own way. LaPorte's spirit is fierce and feisty. Her story is inspiring, her writing lights me up, and she freely admits to her failures, her fears, and her faults. But she's out there changing the world and doing it on her own terms.

Jonathan Fields, author and creator of _Good Life Project_. Fields' rise to fame has been paved with bold decisions (that some viewed as crazy), big transitions, and a lot of passion. It's his compassion, though, that really inspires me. His goal is to help people create businesses that nourish them financially AND spiritually. He sees a new and better way to do business by supporting those brave enough to wade into entrepreneurial waters.

Leo Babauta, blogger at Zenhabits.net and author of the _Power of Less_, belongs on this list, too. Babauta's thoughtful and honest blog helps people make very small changes that lead to big shifts in life. His insightful writing and way of minimalist living (with a wife and a bunch of kids) serves as an example of fully living what he preaches.

Chris Guillebeau, author of the _Art of Nonconformity_ ("Set your own rules, live the life you want and change the world"), charted his course by traveling to every country in the world. He created the World Domination Summit, a series of _Unconventional Guides_ to help people chart their own paths, and wrote two books (_The $100 Start Up_ and _Born for This_). His compassion, thoughtfulness, and way of thinking serve as a wonderful model for someone who consistently wants to serve others.

Kim Dinan and Brian Patton saved up money for two years, sold everything they owned, and traveled the world. They write individual blogs at www.So-Many-Places.com and www.WanderingSasquatch.com and are creating courses to help others go explore the world, too. Right now, they've settled down to raise baby Juniper, but I suspect more adventures await them in the future. Their bravery to answer the call of _"there's GOT to more to life than this"_ is truly inspiring.

Srinivas Rao, creator of _The Unmistakable Creative Podcast,_ is so open about his struggles while simultaneously finding the most interesting people to interview. Their conversations are raw, interesting, and I learn a ton listening to them. His new book brings together many of the lessons he's learned from growing his podcasting business and writing 1,000 words a day unfailingly for several years.

I'm sure there are plenty of other folks who inspire me and who have supported me in helping me to be bold, brave, and taking some action (even if I'm scared shitless while doing it).

Bonus Action Step: make a list of people who inspire YOU. Read their stories again and see if you can discover the steps in their Hero's Journeys. My bet is you'll feel more connected to and inspired by them.

Ways to make some room

So, let's talk about being scared shitless (or what more refined people might call "feeling the FEAR").

Most people admit they feel the fear...some succeed in doing "it" anyway. I have recently learned the most successful ones who plunge ahead and do it anyway have a secret—they've learned to manage their breath.

In her newest book, *Diana, Herself*, author Martha Beck notes, "Humans are one of the few nonaquatic mammals that can voluntarily change the pace of respiration. Rapid breathing is part of the fight-or-flight reaction; slow breathing is part of the relaxation response."

You can learn to manage your breath and thus move from fight-or-flight into deliberate relaxation.

Here's how:

Step One: <u>Breathe</u>! There's an old saying: *fear is simply excitement without breath.* Turn your fear into excitement (relaxed excitement, though) by remembering to breathe!

Several deep breaths will get you started. Remember to breathe starting from your chest and moving down into your abdomen. Pooch your stomach out! In fact, think of your abdomen like a ball—as you breathe, you want to fill that ball with air. Then slowly release.

After a few deep breaths, move into deliberate breathing. Breathe in for five seconds, concentrating on the air moving into your nostrils, into your chest, and down into your belly. Then reverse, concentrating on the air moving through your nose as you empty your belly and chest.

Step Two: <u>Act</u>! Once you've mastered breath, it's time to act! I subscribe to the *Ready? Fire! Aim!* way of living life. Decide what you want to do and simply begin. One of my favorite authors, Seth Godin, talks about making your art and shipping it. And doing it over and over whether you fail or succeed. Nike also advises: *Just Do It.*

Step Three: <u>Be present to the moment you're in</u>. Don't remember the past with fear. Don't future-cast by telling stories. Focus. Pay attention to the here and now. If you're safe, keep breathing and being in the moment. If something is no longer safe, keep breathing (because this is the moment you'll try to hold your breath) and take action until you are physically safe again.

Practice these three steps daily. Or moment-by-moment if you have to. With practice, you will soon find yourself about to be "in the present moment" more and more often and more and more easily.

ACTION STEP

Learning to manage your breath is the key to life. Breathe from your chest and moving down into your abdomen. Pooch your stomach out! In fact, think of your abdomen like a ball—as you breathe, you want to fill that ball with air. Then slowly release.

Next, move into deliberate breathing. Breathe in for five seconds, concentrating on the air moving into your nostrils, into your chest, and down into your belly. Then reverse. Concentrate on moving the air through your nose as you empty your belly and chest. Repeat slowly.

A Note from Nelson about *Be bold. Be brave. Take action. Even if you're scared shitless while doing it.*

What the hell have I done? What will happen to my business? Can I really do this?

Many years ago, I worked as a raft guide, organizing and leading multi-day trips on the New River in West Virginia. That was the beginning of my dream to row the Colorado River through the Grand Canyon. This dream seemed to fade into the back of my mind as life started screaming by, but it was never entirely lost. It would surface from time-to-time, and I would promise myself, "One day I am going to do this."

Twenty-five years (+/-) later, I got an email inviting Angie and me to go on a sixteen-day, 225-mile private rafting trip through Grand Canyon. I do not think we even talked about it. We both looked at each other and said, "We are going!"

For this trip, I was just going along for the ride with hopes of getting to row a little bit of the river. I was also starting to schedule my work around the trip while trying to figure out how to walk away from a growing business for three weeks and have something to return to.

To my surprise, it all came together; even my biggest customer at the time said, "Nelson, the work will be here when you get back."

Then I got an email asking if I wanted to be an oarsman on the trip. My own boat!

Once again, I said yes without thinking. It was a dream come true! But a week or so later, after watching videos of rafters running the big rapids in the Canyon, I had to ask myself, "What have I done? Can I do this? I could die. Am I nuts?"

Several weeks later I sat down on a large gray raft, just like one I had spent many days on 25 (+/-) years ago. I grabbed the oars, and let all my training and experience take over. Confident but scared shitless, Angie and I floated out into the adventure of a lifetime.

Vulcan's Anvil, photo courtesy of Jenni Miehle

Chapter 8: Laugh often and loudly.

There's a thing that everyone waits for on a rafting trip through Grand Canyon. That thing is big, gnarly, and gives pause to even the most experienced oarsmen.

That thing is Lava Rapid.

Lava is a Class TEN rapid and is perhaps the most dreaded rapid on the whole trip.

I could feel the tension build as we got closer to Lava. We camped upstream the night before so we would be fresh and ready for the challenge the next day.

As we geared up the next morning, people were quiet. Solemn. Respectful of the enormous thing we were about to do. There was nervous laughter and only a little mindless chatter.

As we floated downstream, we saw our landmark—the thing that told us we were very close. Vulcan's Anvil is a gigantic black volcanic rock on river right. A rock that is so sacred to Native Americans that we were instructed not to touch it.

I said a prayer to Vulcan's Anvil for our safety as we floated by.

Just before Lava, we eddied out on river left. Oarsmen and kayakers scrambled out of boats and headed downstream to scout the rapid.

The gods were smiling upon us today—we'd be running Lava Rapid at a level that allowed us to take "the sneak." We were running the left side of the rapid, far from the angry, foaming, frothing holes on river right and far from the rock known as "the cheese grater."

After scouting, we watched another group set up to enter the rapids. One-by-one, they launched, most of their group choosing the same left side run we planned. A few ran the right, and we saw one boat flip, its now-displaced (and very wet) occupants swimming like carp to get safely reunited with their raft.

Finally, it was our group's turn. We lined up in an order that took experience and safety into account. One-by-one, each boat entered the rapid. In the froth and roar of that whitewater, Nelson and I hit one rock that spun us around, and then the whole thing was over before I had a chance to even think about counting.

Very quickly we turned around to see the rest of our group have successful runs. One more rapid and a very big dousing of water later, we all gathered on river right at "Tequila Beach."

The mood was euphoric. Everyone took a big swig of tequila from the bottle being passed around. "We did it!" Dancing, smiles, and general ebullience were the name of the game here. We expelled all that nervous energy onto the beach with our laughter, and it turned into sweet relief.

Arriving at our campsite later that afternoon, people put on costumes and decorated the beach for an official "Alive Below Lava" after party. We laughed often and loudly, told jokes, drank more tequila, and generally praised the river gods for sparing us on that fine, sunny day.

Beyond the Canyon

I love my dad. And one of the things I love most about him is his laugh. It is loud. Really loud. When he thinks something is funny, EVERYONE knows it.

Thing is, I'm just like him.

And one of my best friends in the whole world is the same way, too.

Get two or three of us together for a movie or comedy show and people suddenly start staring and/or moving away from us with haste.

We laugh. A lot. Loudly. And without apology.

But I'll admit it wasn't always that way.

There was a time I felt embarrassment and shame about my loud laugh. I'd catch people looking sideways at me and feel judged by them, like I'd done something offensive or wrong.

The very wise Brené Brown, researcher, storyteller, and author of *Daring Greatly* and *Rising Strong*, talks about shame in detail. She says that three things are needed for shame to thrive: judgement, secrecy, and silence. And there's an important difference between guilt (your actions are wrong) and shame (you are wrong). When you think to yourself "Who do I think I am?" or you tell yourself you'll never be good enough, shame is alive and well in you.

For a long time, that shame of being "too loud" or "too much" kept me from laughing my laugh. It made me feel vaguely embarrassed by my dad's loud laugh.

To use a phrase I love, I didn't allow myself to "let my freak flag fly" because I was afraid of being judged for this thing that was part of me, but that wasn't part of, or even accepted by, everyone else.

So, let's talk about you...what's your thing? What your version of "laughing loudly"?

What's the thing about you that's bold, aggressive, obvious, loud, or unique...yet you find yourself apologizing for, trying to tone it down, or explaining it away in embarrassment or shame?

Maybe you like to wear your hair big. Or you shave your legs (and you're a guy). Or perhaps you're quiet—a true introvert—and big social settings send you running far away, fast.

On the surface, laughing loudly and often is about finding time for joy and pleasure, but it's also about accepting and loving the whole of who you are.

And I seriously mean all of you—flaws, quirks, and kooky habits.

I laugh loudly and often. I could be seriously embarrassed by it...or I could (and do) just embrace this quirk and laugh naturally when I find something is funny.

I can't encourage you enough to be your very real self. It brings me so much joy when people can be their authentic selves.

If we really love ourselves and know we are worthy, we don't feel the need for outside approval; we don't explain or apologize for who or what we are.

Our divine nature comes from our humanity and our imperfections, says the marvelous poet David Whyte.

And if your quirkiness has both of us laughing often and loudly together, then all the better.

Get out there and strut your stuff. Fly your freak flag proudly and share the whole of YOU with the whole world.

Ways to make some room

If you've lived in shame of this "thing" of yours, now's the time to begin discovering how to embrace it.

By eliminating your hatred, fear, and loathing of this "thing" that is part of you, you are making some room for love, acceptance, and tolerance for yourself.

Grab a pen and start writing:

My thing is:_____

The negative emotions I feel about it are:

_____
_____
_____
_____

The positive emotions I want to feel about it are:

_____
_____
_____
_____

Next, see how you can begin to catch yourself each time you begin to think that negative thought. Go back to your list and choose a more positive thought. Practice thinking and/or saying that positive thing out loud. Choose a trusted friend to practice with. Soon, you will replace that negative chatter with positive, accepting praise.

Well done! Let's laugh often and loudly together, shall we?

ACTION STEP

Choose that thing about yourself that bugs you. Spend some time with it. Go through the exercise on the previous page.

Enroll a friend and do this exercise together. See how you can support each other in accepting these weird, odd, and kooky things about yourselves!

Chapter 9: Reclaim your nights and weekends. #UNPLUG

After our Grand Canyon trip, Nelson and I returned home to a mountain of mail. Lots of junk, too many credit card offers (feh!), and a bill or three.

My favorite part of the mail is receiving magazines. I don't subscribe to many, but I love the ones I get. Inc. Magazine, Mother Earth News, Fast Company, and Our State (a North Carolina magazine).

On this day, upon returning from such a life-changing adventure, it was the feature story on the cover of Fast Company that grabbed my attention:

> *#UNPLUG: My life was crazy. So I disconnected for 25 days. You should too.*

Egads! I sat with the glorious truth of having just disconnected for sixteen days during our trip. No smartphone, no email, no internet service of ANY kind. No plumbing or electricity (I'll spare you the details on the plumbing). If I needed a light, I either used my headlamp or the moonlight (which was brilliantly full toward the end of our trip).

Flipping to the Fast Company article, I read that the interviewee was a guy who was very involved in EVERY social media outlet possible. His online presence was HUGE.

You, gentle reader, may not be quite so connected. It doesn't mean, however, that you don't relate to his reasons for wanting to unplug:

- His life was crazy busy—24/7 crazy busy.
- He was fully connected to everything and everybody, especially through social media.
- He wanted to be free of obligations, most of which were asserted in some way in digital fashion.
- He needed a mental break.
- He wondered if things would continue without his involvement (meaning he could "do less" after he returned from this break).

Can you relate, even a little bit?

Beyond the Canyon

If you think about it, many (most?) of the requests for your time, your money, and your energy come to you digitally or electronically (email, text, phone, social media).

Suffice it to say, it's stressing you out (I say this as a statement of fact for many of us). It's distracting you. And it also may be leading you to suffer, consciously or unconsciously, from FOMO (Fear of Missing Out).

I know you are checking email in the middle of meetings or in the middle of the night or as your employees (or spouses, partners, or children) are trying to talk to you. You're listening to voicemails or reading texts while you're driving (or at best while stopped at red lights). Your phone comes out in the middle of dinner with your family. And sadly, instead of reaching for the person sleeping beside you, you reach for your personal devices (tablet, laptop, smartphone) as soon as your eyes pop open in the morning, right?

You fear missing out on:

- the next big deal
- the next big potential client
- the newest news
- a call or email from The Really Angry Client (we have to be responsive, don't we?)
- an "inside scoop" or office gossip
- being "in the know"
- a promotion or the next great offer
- what your own brain might come up with
- what your inner voice might want to share with you

Those last two might actually be more avoidance than fear of missing out, but you get the picture.

Let's talk about a digital detox.

The saturation of digital connectedness in our lives is epidemic. And I assert it's unhealthy if we just "let it happen," like waves of information lapping over heads, threatening with each new surge to drown us.

The good news is there are ways to regain control and reclaim your sanity. As the Dog Whisperer, Cesar Milan, would say, "We must embrace rules, boundaries, and limitations." It's the only way to beat back the crazies.

Truth is, though, we've forgotten how to unplug. Check out. Be still. Do nothing. I believe we've even forgotten what it means to be bored.

And frankly, the stress of this is making us sick and miserable. And for some, it's killing us.

#UNPLUG

Part of my mission in life is to encourage EVERYONE to unplug, check out, be still, and do nothing, even if for just a few minutes each day.

I know, I know, unplugging sounds scary—after all, the reality is you suffer from FOMO. Plus, your devices are *designed* to grab your attention. Did you know you get a hit of dopamine from each buzz, beep, ding, ring, and vibration? And the dopamine reward has deepened your habit and created a reward cycle in your brain that IS an addiction. When you hear/feel your device, someone else's, OR just imagine you do (called Phantom Vibration Syndrome), you still get that hit of dopamine. Conversely, all that buzzing, beeping, dinging, and ringing causes a rise in cortisol (the "fight or flight" hormone). Too much cortisol, though, makes your adrenal glands wear out quickly. With all the up and down of your hormones, over time, your health truly begins to suffer.

Additionally, you might begin to notice you feel "naked" without your device, vulnerable to the "big, bad world." And as a status symbol, your device might become part of your identity (like an extra appendage or a crutch)—something you unconsciously use to avoid downtime or conversation, or to bond with others ("Look, I have the newest, latest, greatest, coolest iPhone").

And the issue isn't going away. In fact, our screens and devices are becoming more pervasive every single year. According to a July 2012 issue of Newsweek called "Tweets, Texts, E-mail and Posts: Is the Onslaught Making Us Crazy," here are a few facts to get your attention:

- On average, Americans stare at some type of computer screen for eight hours a day (more time than we spend on any other activity including sleeping).
- Teens fit some seven hours of screen time into the average school day; eleven, if you count time spent multi-tasking on several devices.
- When President Obama ran for office in 2008, the iPhone had just been introduced.
- Smartphones outnumber regular ones, and more than a third of users check their smartphones before they even get out of bed.
- The average person, regardless of age, sends or receives about 400 text messages a month—four times the 2007 number.

- The average teen processes an astounding 3,700 texts a month, double the 2007 figure.
- More than two thirds of normal, everyday people report feeling their phones vibrate when, in fact, nothing is happening with their phone (researchers call it "phantom-vibration syndrome").

Peter Whybrow, the director of the Semel Institute for Neuroscience and Human Behavior at UCLA, argues that the computer is like "electronic cocaine" for certain groups of people.

He likens our newly-evolving relationship with the computer to an out-of-control horse which has rapidly left the building of its own accord, taking the unwilling rider (us) with it. The unbridled use of technology can fuel cycles of hyper-manic behavior followed by periods of depression.

But rather than ignore this rapidly evolving technology that most all us of have to use every single day, Whybrow encourages us to realize this is a totally new thing. And unless we figure out how to manage and control both the computer and our use of it, then we are at great risk. Some people will have minor scrapes (fatigue, overuse, overwhelm) and others will have more severe consequences (burnout, relational issues, and even full-blow addictions). This applies not just to our computers, but to all the electronic devices that we interact with.

What's the solution?

I'm so glad you asked...

Rules, boundaries, limitations

According to R. Skip Johnson's article "Setting Boundaries and Setting Limits," personal boundaries are about setting safe, permissible and reasonable limits. Our boundaries become rules and guidelines to let people know where our limits are. They become a mixture of attitudes and built on what we've learned and experienced. Boundaries work both ways as we interact with others and as they interact with us. I also believe we would be wise begin adding boundaries around how we use our technology and how our technology tries to "use" us.

Down deep in the Canyon, we couldn't have plugged in even if we wanted to. It was a gift that the only electronic device we had was a satellite phone for emergencies.

Push vs. pull

Your devices are designed to default to a "PUSH" functionality. This means they automatically want to push information, sounds, alerts, badges, and notifications *at* you.

My advice to save your sanity? *Turn them OFF.*

Turn off the bings, dings, buzzes, vibrations, and visual alerts. This way, you make the choice to engage thoughtfully with the devices instead of those devices interrupting you continuously with their artificial urgency and neediness.

Don't just think about your phone. Think about all your devices:

- smartphone
- tablet
- laptop
- desktop
- televisions (watch out—they are becoming smarter!)

Get into a routine of checking them just a few times a day, for as little time as possible. Pull information *toward* you when you need it, rather than being overwhelmed by it being pushed at you all the time.

Think about your routines

The biggest take-away here is: *do not be complacent*. Do not use these devices unconsciously. Choose, decide, and set some rules, boundaries, and limitations for evenings, weekends, and group events.

Choose, decide, and set some rules, boundaries, and limitations on the alerts, reminders, bings, dings, and buzzes that happen on your devices.

This puts YOU back in control.

Ways to make some room

Here are some suggestions that have helped me:

- When I am with someone, I keep my phone in my purse. I put the ringer on silent. If I am expecting a call, I will alert the person I'm with that if the phone rings, I will only take that one call.

- During a meal with others, I focus on the people I'm with and leave my phone in my purse. I prefer to enjoy their company and the conversation.
- At night, I have my phone scheduled to "sleep" between the hours of 10 p.m. and 7 a.m. I won't get any alerts or notifications (though I've turned almost all of those off anyway).
- During vacation, limiting "screen time" can be a healthy way to "unplug." My husband and I post photos to our Facebook page (YukonandBean) but otherwise limit our time checking social media or email.
- Stretch goal: completely turn off your devices on the weekends!

Make it your mission in life to #UNPLUG with some regularity. Turn it into a habit and see how your life and your relationships improve because of it.

ACTION STEP

Simple: #UNPLUG

Try it for an evening or even for an entire weekend.

Chapter 10: Busy is a bullshit word. Stop saying it. Choose to say something real.

While we were on the river, navigating rapids especially, there were times when we were fast, furious, and focused. In the Canyon, we did what we had to do in the moment (navigate a tough rapid, unload boats, and set up camp, prep, and serve meals). But after each flurry of fast, furious focus, we settled back in to the rhythm of the river. I wouldn't call the fast, furious, focused time "busy," though. We were purposeful, engaged, and in tune with our surroundings.

Someone might not be available to help you right this second because they are engaged in some other task, but no one was "busy just to be busy." We were either purposefully "doing" or we were sitting and relaxing, taking advantage of the much-needed downtime between chores, rapids, exploring, and rest.

There was no mindless surfing the internet, checking email, or worrying about what was happening on social media. No one created busy work just to be moving. It was perfectly acceptable to sit do nothing when there nothing to be done.

Basically, we had two options:

1. We were "ON" (focused on the task at hand)
2. We were "OFF" (resting, chatting, restoring our energy for our next "ON" cycle)

When I think about how we lived and worked on the Canyon versus how we live and work at home, the difference is striking.

Without our devices, we weren't artificially overstimulated. Our brains weren't constantly searching for the next/new/important thing or being fearful about missing out on some seemingly important thing.

We just existed in that canyon with each other and with nature.

For instance, if we didn't have cooking or Groover duties, we took care of personal needs. Instead of staring at screens, some of us stared in wonder at the sky, the water, and the incredible walls that never seemed to end in Grand Canyon. Others sat quietly and journaled or read books. Some snuck away to bathe in the very refreshing (read: FREEZING) cold water or to lay in the shade and nap. Some laced up boots and hiked to see pictographs, amazing views, or roaring waterfalls. Most of us did all those things at points along the trip.

But there was no mindless activity. We were either purposefully ON or we were OFF resting.

There was no "busy" for sake of being busy. We didn't seek out things to fill the time. Most of us were satisfied to relax and sit when we had the time (partly because we were exhausted, but partly because there was nothing else urging us to "go, do, acquire, learn").

Beyond the Canyon

I noticed something happening several years ago: everyone was walking around saying how "busy" they were. They walked fast, talked fast, and seemed really stressed out.

When someone tells me how busy they are, I ask follow up questions: "So, business is booming?" or "Is life just terrific?" By and large the honest answer is a sheepish "I wish!"

Then I read several articles that referenced the "Cult of Busy." People wore their overwhelm like a badge and proudly discussed how many hours they put in at work, at night, and even throughout the weekend.

Perhaps *you* are card-carrying member of the "Cult of Busy." Maybe in your social circles, being busy is seen as a positive thing, something to be glorified, or rewarded.

I wonder, though, when the last time was anyone handed out an award for "Busiest Business Person of the Year"?

Ick!

So, what does being "busy" really mean?

Frankly, I believe busy is a bullshit word. It's filler language, like saying, "I'm fine" when you're really truly not. "Busy" is meaningless and vague.

Harvard economist Juliet Shore, wrote in *The Overworked American* that our parents and grandparents got 50 percent less work done per hour than us, AND they had more leisure time. So, even if we simply cut back, we'd fine we have more time to do things we love.

Shore believes we are addicted to work (out of fear of losing our jobs OR out of fear of what we would do to fill the time if we weren't at work).

Here's what I think is happening: "busy" is our safe word. Our go-to answer. It's a cop-out; a way to sound like we're rocking and rolling and making it happen when in reality it's a cover up, a sham, or a farce.

After my Grand Canyon trip, when I shared the *Make Some Room Manifesto* with my friends and across social media, one of my readers wrote back with this:

Angie,

This manifesto hangs on our refrigerator.

My husband and I have adopted "Busy is a Bullshit Word." We say it every day, either to ourselves when we need to make choices about what to commit to, or about other people when they say they are too busy to hold up their end of an agreement they made with us.

It's changing our lives.

Elizabeth

BAM! That's exactly what I'm talking about. Busy is a cover up. A way to make an excuse without being specific. A way to keep people at arm's length. To not engage. Or to weasel out of something without actually saying what you mean.

Think about it this way...

When a person says, "I'm fine" in response to a question, what does that really mean?

It either means nothing or, in some cases, it means he or she ain't fine but doesn't want to say so.

Further probing might get the person to admit what's going on; in others, he or she refuses to say so and it becomes a passive-aggressive way to punish people.

Within society, I think some people are using the phrase, "I'm so busy" in the same way.

It might be as an attention-getting behavior ("Oh poor me, I'm soooo busy").

Or it could be a way to deflect having a more real, honest conversation (because things aren't going well at all, and they don't want to discuss it).

Ways to make some room

Now, I don't want or expect people to lay their hearts bare if they are having a hard time. Some things don't need to be shared with the world. But because I believe it's important to be prepared, here are some things you can do instead of using the generic "things are busy:"

- Be honest.
- Be forthright.
- Be specific.

My friend Brooks has been practicing and loving saying, "I'm awesomely full with lots of spaciousness, too."

She also notes, "It's very empowering to choose other words—it's a choice."

Other examples:

- "There's a lot of good flowing in my life/work right now."
- "I have so much potential/possibility to choose from..."

- "I've got lots of pots brewing these days..."

By saying what you mean, asking for what you need, and being specific with your language, you can begin to live in a transparent and honest world. It becomes easy to communicate with you and people know they can trust you.

ACTION STEP

Banish "busy" from your vocabulary. It will change how you feel about your life. And it can create the opportunity for deeper conversation and connection between you and the person/people you're with.

Chapter 11: Keep only the useful, beautiful, and joyful.

I brought too many clothes and too many shoes on my Grand Canyon trip because I wasn't totally sure what I'd need. I packed for "just in case" scenarios. In the end, I wore the same bathing suit the entire trip (yes, I washed it). I rotated through three shirts during the days and pretty much wore the same thing to bed each night. I wore the same pair of pants each day until they tore apart during a hike. I wore my SmartWool socks and my Chaco sandals every single day—even for hiking. I had extra shirts, shorts, bathing suits, flip flops, and a pair of hiking shoes. Turns out, I didn't need any of them.

The one thing I was happy to have two of was sunglasses. I broke my first pair just a few days into the trip. It would have been miserable if I hadn't brought along the second pair.

But the rest of it? I could have saved myself the effort of lugging it through several airports, paying for the weight of it all, and lugging it around campsites each time we loaded and unloaded the boats for sixteen days straight.

Beyond the Canyon

> *"Have nothing in your houses that you do not know to be useful or believe to be beautiful."*
>
> —William Morris

I want to expand on this most wonderful quote and apply it not only to your home but to your workplace, your work space, and everywhere in between.

(I can apply it even to the stuff I packed for the river trip.)

Our lives are overstuffed. Oversaturated. Overdone. Complicated. Complex. And I suspect it's only happened in the last 100 years as we've added technology, travel, cheap consumer goods, and a lot of choices.

Let me be clear: I'm not trying to advocate that we go back to pioneer days when everyone owned one change of clothes and a spoon. What I am advocating for is making your life simpler—a LOT simpler—in order to focus on the useful, beautiful, and joyful.

Right now, in the USA, we live in a throw-away society. Items we buy at certain stores are meant to have a short life—they're made overseas with cheap materials and with the idea that you'll buy the item, use it a bit until it breaks or wears out, and then you'll head back to the store to buy a replacement doodad (and maybe some additional things you didn't even know you needed until you walked around the store).

We live in a consumer society where shopping and buying are encouraged. Commercials are everywhere, on our TVs, personal devices, radios, and websites.

Buy new, buy more, buy now, buy, buy, buy!

The slick marketing assures you that you'll be happier, more satisfied, and surely more successful if you own or drive the latest and greatest, right?

Is that true though?

Suffering from overabundance

Despite our affluence and overabundance of stuff, studies prove that we are a deeply unhappy nation of people.

In her book *Paris Letters,* author Janice McLeod saved a bunch of money, reduced her belongings down to a single suitcase, and quit her job. Off she went to travel the world.

In the process of reducing and simplifying her life, she realized she had real freedom to explore, roam, and be. The elimination of choice set her free.

It's also a lot easier to decide what to wear each morning when you have deliberately limited your choices.

Professional Organizer Marie Kondo wrote a whole book about simplifying called *The Life-Changing Magic of Tidying Up*. It has one abiding principle: Does this thing bring you joy? If not, get rid of it (and/or stop doing it).

Out on the river for sixteen days, there weren't a lot of choices about what to wear or what to eat. The flipside was tons of time for exploring, having conversations, or just *being*.

The modern life

Consider that in 1975, the average size of a house (in the U.S.) was 1,525 square feet. By 2013, that number jumped to 2,598 square feet. Research shows people (especially in first world countries) are experiencing "consumer fatigue." People are literally tired of buying stuff! They are tired of dusting, organizing, and managing stuff they've already accumulated.

In his book *Stuffocation*, researcher Tom Gilovich talks about "adaptation." He discusses how new purchases often make us feel very happy, but once we get used to the new thing, our happiness levels plummet because the thing becomes a normal, uneventful part of our lives (in other words, it fades into the background as we adapt to seeing or using the thing). He notes that purchasing things doesn't make us happy long-term, but experiential-type purchases do.

For me, collecting experiences instead of things is my number one priority.

Ways to make some room

If you aren't sure how to simplify your life or your stuff, here are a myriad of ways to help you simplify:

- What's on your desk? Visual clutter is so distracting!
- Declutter your space—less to dust, less to clean.
- Get stuff OFF your to-do list—you're not getting to a lot of it anyway, right?
- Clear out your brain—hello, Monkey Mind! (You know: the endless chatter that fills our heads, drowns our hearts, and starves our souls.)
- Reduce your clothes, shoes, accessories—fewer choices means fewer decisions. Keeping only what you LOVE and WEAR simplifies your mornings. Yes, this means you'll wear your clothes more often—people will see you in the same clothes a lot. So?
- Declutter your morning and evening routines—start your day calmly and with conscious choices. End your day with stillness and connection to yourself and your family.
- Get rid of books, CDs, DVDs and even that old record collection. Keep only what you use and love. Everything else is you living in the past or worrying about the future. Be here now—keep what you use now.
- Clients, customers, projects—yes, fire them if they are a pain in the ass, abusive to you or your staff, aren't bringing you satisfaction, or if they aren't making you money (and especially if they are making you LOTS of money but are one of the first three things I mentioned). Pain in the ass clients who are disrespectful, mean, late for

appointments, late to pay, etc. ARE NOT WORTH THE ENERGY OR TIME OR MONEY. You're kidding yourself if you think they are (especially if it's about money).

- Get rid of PAPER! Seriously, when was the last time you looked at half of what you're keeping? Unless you need it for legal or tax reasons or you're actively using it for a project, get rid of it!
- Reduce the sentimental stuff. If it's sentimental (photos, books, kids artwork) do you need to keep it all? Can you pare it down to a few treasured pieces? Can you digitize any of it? Remember—it isn't about the "thing" it's about the emotion the "thing" makes you FEEL.
- Throw out or donate food you won't/can't/should not be eating. Past the expiration? Toss it. Didn't like it? Donate it. It's crap? Throw it away (or if unopened and you have the receipt, return it).
- Cleaning products are clutter. Often we just have too much. And [rant alert] most of these products are poisons. You can do A LOT with baking soda, vinegar, and essential oils.
- Art—does it still bring you joy? If it doesn't sell it, donate it, or give it away. Just because it used be "awesome" doesn't mean you're stuck with it for life!
- Stuff related to hobbies—are you still actively participating! Great—keep what you use and get rid of the rest. Not doing the hobby anymore? You're living in the past—time to bless it, release it, and free up the space (mentally and physically) for something NEW.
- Office supplies—when the sticky notes are so old the sticky is gone, it's time to start throwing stuff

away! Envelopes, business cards, pens, pencils, office machines, dried up white out, rubber bands that are dry and rotted, old folders...the list goes on.

ACTION STEP

Go through the list above. CIRCLE IN RED the ones you're committed to simplifying in your life. Then, pull out your calendar and schedule one hour (each day, each week, or each month) to purge each area you circled.

Chapter 12: We cannot know it all, read it all, keep it all, do it all, have it all, or be it all. And that's actually a good thing.

Our Grand Canyon trip was the ultimate practice of "less is more:"

- Take only what you need; leave everything else behind.
- Study the description of the rapid in the books and handouts. Walk down the riverbank and scout the rapid. See your lines and choose the one that looks "best" to you. "Best" on the river can mean safest, least risky, or even most fun.
- Choose a campsite suitable for number of folks on the trip; preferably one that is situated on the side of the Canyon that will either be sunniest longest (for a winter trip) or get shady soonest (important

when you're there in June and the high hits 107 degrees).

- Set up your kitchen, sleeping area, and personal items before it gets dark. Be alert for critters (ants, scorpions, snakes, ravens) and protect your gear from their teeth and beaks. Rodents are notorious for chewing through bags to get to food and other tasty items; ravens will unzip or undo anything that looks tempting or shiny. And ants, scorpions, and snakes? Just stay alert—they can hurt!
- Consult your recipe list and open the coolers as little as possible to retrieve the food you need. Making ice last for sixteen days is no easy task!
- Follow the recipes for the best outcome based on the ingredients given. Hungry people don't care about fancy food—they just want something tasty and filling at the end of a long day!

This idea of not knowing it all, reading it all, keeping it all, doing it all, having it all, or being it all is never truer than on an expedition trip like the Grand Canyon. There simply isn't room for everything you might want to bring. You can't do all the side trips available. You can't read everything about the Canyon before you go. And you certainly can't "be it all" out there. Especially during a single sixteen-day trip.

Beyond the Canyon

An organizing client of mine shared with me that he subscribed to a dozen different magazines and several newspapers and had at least 100 books on his shelves (with probably a third that he hadn't read yet). When I asked him how he found time to consume all this material, he confessed he couldn't but held onto it all with a desperate hope to "someday" find the time. I jokingly suggested he take a speed-reading course.

Remember how the feminists of the 70s said, "*You can have it all!*" as their rallying cry?

Oh, how things have changed! Today, I think people—especially women—are desperately trying NOT to have to know it all, read it all, keep it all, do it all, have it all, or be it all, despite advertising and a culture that says, "Say YES to it all!"

As a society, we're exhausted, sleep deprived, in debt, and overscheduled to the max.

Figuring out what to let go of is a life-saving and sanity-retaining skill.

Giving yourself permission to stop trying to do it all is the first step.

Maybe your thinking goes, "If it shows up in my life (or in my email, at my door, in my mailbox, or on my desk), it must be important and I should jump on it, right?"

WRONG.

This is where you get to be **discerning**. (Remember back in Chapter 6 where I talked about being discerning?)

The definition of discerning is: *being able to see and understand people, things, or situations clearly.*

Discerning is about **choosing**. It's being present in the moment, making a judgment call, and choosing the best available option *for you*.

Why being discerning is SO hard

In Rick Hanson's April 2016 edition of *Wise Brain Bulletin*, Editor Michael Taft notes that we are full of ideas, concepts, and experiences that we can do nothing about. We can't turn them into anything because of limited time, attention, energy, etc. Problem is, we keep refreshing our need to seek information. And we do it because we're looking for that hit of dopamine that makes us feel so good. But even too much of a good thing it still too much. He refers to it as our "brain being full."

Does this sound horrible to you? Out of control? Acting on the whim of our hormones?

Let's hit the STOP button. Take a step back. And take a few deeps breaths.

We cannot know it all, read it all, keep it all, do it all, have it all, or be it all. And that's actually a good thing because it actually means we can *stop trying*.

What if there was another way? A better way?

I beg you to start making conscious choices. In every area of your life:

- what you eat
- volunteer opportunities

- what's in your closet
- anything you buy (but before you buy it)
- work promotions
- job opportunities
- life partners/dating
- whether to have pets or not
- stuff clogging up your inbox and snail mail box
- things in your kitchen
- bins and boxes in your attic/garage
- where you live
- whether you are active or not
- what you read
- what you watch
- what you listen to
- what kind of car you drive
- medicines you might or might not take
- what you hold onto
- books on your shelves
- pictures on your walls
- shoes on your feet
- ANYTHING/EACH THING in your life represents a choice

Ways to make some room

Before you stuff your brain, your schedule, your home, or even your bag full of "important stuff," turn on your discernment switch:

- Is everything essential?
- If not, what can be removed?

- Does this choice serve only me or the greater whole (partnership, family, community, and world)?
- Is there a different choice?
- Is there a better choice?
- Does this clarify things?
- Is it the right time to take action?
- Is there a simpler choice?
- Does this *feel* right to you?

Are you drinking from a fire hose of life?
Take a minute and think about that visual—you, drinking from a fire hose.

OUCH!

Let's deliberately turn down the flow and try drinking from the garden hose instead.

(See your Action Step on the next page.)

ACTION STEP

What activities can you purposefully and thoughtfully remove from your to-do list?

- people pleasing
- obsessively checking email over and over and over
- multi-tasking
- saying "yes" to everything, always without thought
- reacting to all messages (email, voicemail, text, snail mail)
- doing it all
- not getting enough sleep, exercise, sex
- perfectionism ("Shitty first drafts" are awesome! Thanks, Anne Lamott.)
- skipping meals
- not taking time to pee, stretch, or otherwise get away from your desk during the day
- getting bogged down needing to know it all before starting
- getting stuck because you don't know "how"
- holding your breath (here's a secret: breath is LIFE)
- procrastinating (UNLESS it's part of your process)
- doing all the little "safe" stuff before tackling the big "risky" stuff
- apologizing (ladies—this might be for you)
- fitting in "one more thing" before heading out the door
- ignoring your Soul's calling
- hiding, shrinking
- boasting, faking
- doing laundry instead of your "Right Work"
- staring at your phone instead of being present with the person in front of you
- avoiding the difficult conversations (tip: five seconds of discomfort now instead of five months of resentment later)

Chapter 13: Kill your microwave. Throw out your TV.

Obviously, we were without televisions and microwaves for the whole of our Canyon trip. Most everything we ate was made from scratch, using fresh and frozen ingredients. We ate normal foods (burgers, steaks, chops, spaghetti, and brownies, though not all at the same time.)

Toward the end of the trip, food got a tiny bit monotonous, especially at breakfast, because we chose "cold" options (like bagels with lox and cream cheese, yogurt, and cereal) rather than "hot" breakfasts of bacon, eggs, and pancakes.

That being said, with everyone being assigned to help cook, we ate like kings.

And what did we do when we weren't on a cook team? With no TV to "veg out" in front of, we took hikes, made time for bathing, or just sat in our chairs and watched the water roll by.

Were we bored?

Never. Not once.

Beyond the Canyon

I will preface this part by saying this section of the book is more of a personal rant about the television and microwave than a literal plea for you to ditch both (unless you want to).

More than anything, my suggestions to kill your microwave and throw out your TV are really to start a discussion about *mindfulness*.

My favorite definition of *mindfulness* is "a mental state achieved by focusing one's awareness on the present moment, while calmly acknowledging and accepting one's feelings, thoughts, and bodily sensations, used as a therapeutic technique."

In un-fancy terms, this just means "being here now." In your body. Feeling your feelings. Present with the people you're with, or present with yourself if you're alone.

One of the greatest gifts of the Canyon was having the time to sit and talk with other people on this trip. To slow down and have real conversation. To realize at times I was tired and needed a break from people. Or that I was just exhausted from the stress of the rapids, the heat, and the sand and needed some quiet time by myself.

Throwing out your microwave

First, let me say there are plenty of credible studies that prove microwaves are safe. And I admit they are handy for heating water for tea or defrosting meat in a hurry.

My issue with the microwave is when it is used to make a fast meal out of "fake" food (think TV dinner loaded with preservatives). Pre-processed convenience foods only serve to disassociate us from the food our bodies want. The microwave allows up to "zap" our food (doesn't that scare anyone else?) and to eat on the run. Fast, fast, fast, go, go, go. The opposite of mindfulness.

And to add insult to injury, a March 2015 Washington Post article called "The Slow Death of the Home Cooked Meal" noted some 60 percent of people microwave their food. We can assume many of them then eat in front of the television. It's a double dose of detachment.

With so many eating disorders, with obesity at epidemic proportions, and depression causing all sorts of issues, I believe being mindful and being in community with one another are the missing links.

Instead, I'm a big fan of the "Slow Food" movement. If you haven't heard of it, check it out. Slow food is about taking time to cook from scratch, at home, alone or with your family and friends, using simple ingredients. I'm also a fan of buying local food from farmers I've met and trust.

Choosing real food (again, hopefully grown locally and possibly organically) and cooking with care is the first step. Whether you're alone, with one other person, or a group of people, choosing an attitude of care (dare I say love) encourages mindfulness.

Suggestions for anyone to create a mindful meal setting (no microwaves required)

Solos: Set a beautiful table. Light a candle. Use cloth napkins and your best dishes. Make it a special event for one. Cook your favorite food(s). Eat slowly. Savor your creation. Enjoy the time deeply.

Introverts: Invite your favorite person to eat a meal with you. Create a scenario that feels good to you—fun and/or meaningful conversation, great music, or your favorite movie or TV show. Cook the food with love and care. Serve it with a flourish that fits your style. Most importantly, be yourself and be comfortable!

Extroverts: Gather around a table to eat, talk, and laugh! Doing this regularly is delightful. And you don't even have to know the people! Nelson and I used to do community Sunday dinners (when we had a bigger table) and sent out an open invitation on Facebook for anyone to come join us. The point was gathering for a good meal and sharing conversation. And if you're worried about starting conversations (with people you know or that you don't), try Danielle LaPorte's *Conversation Starters* app. You'll get to know people very well and fairly quickly using her questions. If you want to be really saucy, start a game of *Cards Against Humanity* (this game requires more than a bit of sass, a lot of crass, and a very good sense of humor).

Let's Talk TV

Do you know what television actually is? It's an electronic device that "tells a Vision." This vision is created, written, and acted out by other people.

I decided years ago I wanted to create my own vision for my life and how I spend my time. So, I canceled my cable subscription and never looked back. This means:

- I've saved roughly $75/month for the last 12 years for a total nearing $10,800.
- I don't mindlessly channel surf.
- I'm not subject to TV commercials trying to convince me to buy things I didn't know existed and that I didn't even know I even wanted (until I watched the commercials).
- I avoid the need to keep up with the (TV) Joneses.
- I'm not told "what I'm missing out on."
- I avoid the rampant fear-mongering on most news shows these days.
- I avoid being bombarded with food and pharmaceutical commercials.
- Not only am I saving a ton of money, I've also found other, more valuable (to me) ways to spend my time (hiking, gardening, reading, even watching carefully chosen documentaries or even a smart, funny series).

Someone close to me likes to point out that I'm not being truthful when I say I don't have a TV. Technically, she's correct—I've always had a TV. Right now, we do have a small TV in our camper. When I lived alone, I had a small 13-inch TV, with rabbit ears and a built-in VCR for watching movies. When I met my husband, he owned a very large 50-inch television. He loves surround sound and watching movies on "the big screen" right there in the living room.

Additionally, we do regularly watch shows and documentaries on streaming services like Amazon Prime and Netflix, and we run them through the television. I've begun saying now we don't have *traditional TV*. We don't subscribe to cable or satellite and our antenna only picks up five or six channels (including a couple PBS stations, which I do love).

Rather than making TV the enemy, the point is we can consciously and deliberately choose what to watch rather than mindlessly filling time with whatever happens to be on, or trying to relieve stress by "checking out" in front of any program that's on.

Ways to make some room

Just a few changes in your TV watching habits can make a big difference. Try these:

- Begin deliberately reducing the amount of time you watch television. An hour or two a day adds up.
- Reduce the number of shows you watch to only the ones you love and that make you feel good.
- When you're feeling really brave and have the family on board, get rid of all but one TV in the house.
- Schedule TV-free days (or weeks or months).
- Cancel your cable or satellite.

- Consider streaming services for shows you do want to watch (this will save you oodles of money).
- When you're really ready to commit, ditch all the TVs.
- Again, focus on activities that don't revolve around watching television. There are too many to list here!

ACTION STEP

Go through the list above. CIRCLE IN RED the ones you (and perhaps your family) are committed to trying. Then, give it a try for a week or a month and see what changes.

Chapter 14: Stop being a mindless consumer (of information, products, and food). Start caring where "it" comes from.

Deep in the Grand Canyon, there was one single opportunity for us to spend money. Around day eight, we stopped for a two-hour break at Phantom Ranch. I bought postcards and ice-cold lemonade. Nelson bought a beer, some postcards, and a couple of stickers. We wrote out postcards to friends and family and added the iconic "Mailed By Mule" stamp.

The rest of the trip we used what we had, traded for what we absolutely needed, or simply went without.

No glass is allowed on Canyon trips, so we had quite a large collection of aluminum cans by the end of our adventure. I wish I'd remembered to count how many bags we ended up with!

For a sixteen-day trip with sixteen people, though, we created a surprisingly small amount of garbage. And with the "pack it in, pack it out" mantra, this was important!

Beyond the Canyon

In addition to not being a mindless consumer (of information, products, and food) and caring where those things you do consume come from, I'd add "start caring where it goes" when you throw it away, too.

The focus on waste and "pack it in, pack it out" got me thinking more about our needs and wants, how the USA is becoming a "disposable nation" and Americans seem to want "more" better, faster, and cheaper (quantity over quality).

When I began looking at recycling and waste around the world, here are a few interesting tidbits I found:

- **Sweden powers a quarter of a million homes with burned up waste. Less than 1 percent of their household garbage ends up in landfills!** (source: http://www.iflscience.com/environment/less-1-swedens-trash-ends-landfills/)

- **Switzerland has a landfill ban. All of their non-recycled combustible waste must be incinerated.** (source: www.un.org)
- **Iceland supplies about 85 percent of its total energy supply from locally produced renewable energy sources, including geothermal energy and hydropower.**(source:https://askjaenergy.com/iceland-introduction/iceland-energy-sector/)
- **Patagonia (the company) uses recycled polyester and only organic (rather than conventional pesticide-intensive) cotton in its clothing.** (source: www.patagonia.com)

In contrast, for 2013, the US only recycled about 34.5 percent of its municipal waste (source: www.resource-recycling.com). We have a LONG way to go to reach Sweden's 99 percent rate.

That being said, there is much you can do to help our environment.

Note: the average American throws away four and a half pounds of garbage every single day (EPA Fact and Figures).

Why does this matter?
Some people say recycling is futile. I say it's better to try and do something than to give up. If each person in the US would change just one habit a year, that would make a HUGE difference.

When we eat local, recycle, and care about what we're buying, we're voting with our dollars. We're making a small dent in the problem, one person at a time.

Ways to make some room

You can do your part:

- Compost your kitchen waste (including egg shells, coffee grounds, tea bags, and fruit and vegetable waste).
- Recycle your mixed paper, glass, and plastic.
- Recycle your aluminum and steel cans.
- Use your curbside drop off! 86 percent (approximately 254 million) of Americans have access to curbside or drop-off paper recycling programs (www.earth911.org). Are you participating in your recycling program? And if you don't have one, are you separating your recyclables anyway and carting them to your nearest recycling center? Sure, it's more of an effort, but it's worth it in the long run!
- When buying in bulk, bring your own re-usable mesh bags instead of using the plastic bags provided.
- Shop local (for example, at your local farmer's market). You reduce the carbon footprint of the food you eat and reduce your exposure to pesticides. Plus, your money stays in the local economy.
- Stop buying bottled water. Bring your own refillable water bottle to the office and to special events. Get your own reusable coffee mug, too!
- Use low-flow toilets and install low-flow showerheads. Turn the tap off as you brush your teeth.
- Buy local—instead of shipping vegetables and fruits across the country (which are water-hogs to grow),

buy what's local and in season. You'll help your local economy, support the small farmers, and potentially eat healthier, too.

- The biggest water saver? Stop eating beef. Seriously. Watch the fantastic documentary *Cowspiracy* to learn more.

ACTION STEP

Go through the list above. CIRCLE IN RED the ones you (and perhaps your family) are committed to trying. Then, give it a try for a week or a month and watch how those changes become habits!

And a final word on all that STUFF:

As a complement to these ideas, there's a great video that talks about the cycle of stuff—how it's made, where it goes, and what happens when it's thrown away. Check it out here: http://StoryofStuff.org/

Chapter 15: Clutter is the inability (or unwillingness) to make a decision. DECIDE.

"Action is the antidote to fear."

—*Shannon Presson*

Way back in the introduction, I talked about "microtrash" in the Canyon. Microtrash is all the crumbs and little bits of plastic, wood, charcoal, cloth, and detritus humans manage to create in the normal course of living.

If everyone who rafted Grand Canyon overlooked microtrash, there would be a HUGE amount of TINY trash clogging up the waters and shores of the Colorado River in a very short amount of time.

Trash was everyone's responsibility. If we saw microtrash, we picked it up and deposited in the day's trash bag. It was the very last thing we did before we left camp every single morning. And it didn't matter if the microtrash was ours or not; if we saw it, we picked it up.

Microtrash in the Canyon is one thing; it becomes harder in regular day-to-day life to handle this kind of stuff.

Beyond the Canyon

In your daily life, clutter might build up because:

1. You cannot decide what to do *with* something.
2. You can't decide what to do *about* something.

For example, you bring in the mail. There's a coupon for a certain thing you'd like to buy. You don't need it now, but you don't want to toss the valuable coupon.

What do you do with it?

Or maybe you have tons of clothes. You wear some and pile them up. You wear some more and pile those up. Soon, you just have a giant pile of clothes cluttering your dresser, room, or even parts of your house.

If we go back to Chapter 11 (Keep only the useful, beautiful, and joyful), you can purposefully solve a lot of your clutter issues by reducing and simplifying the stuff in your life.

When you get ready to reduce and simplify, find questions that spur you into action. Remember Marie Kondo's question: "Does this thing bring me joy?" Your answer should be a clear YES or NO answer. I find it's harder to put off that decision when I have a clear answer (especially when the answer is a clear NO).

Example:

Problem: I have SO many clothes. Some I wear simply because my favorite clothes are dirty (or wrinkled or I can't find them under the pile of my other clothes).

Solution: Hang up your clothes or deposit them in the dirty clothes hamper after you wear them. Develop a habit of doing a load a laundry each week (I do mine every Monday morning).

Solution II: Reduce your clothes to only those things you love and wear all the time. Keep special occasion clothes and season-specific clothes elsewhere. This reduces your choices dramatically and helps you make much faster decisions about what to wear each day.

Solution III: Be like Steve Jobs, Mark Zuckerberg, and Barack Obama. They each have a very limited amount of clothing to choose from, which makes for quick and easy decision-making in this area.

- black turtlenecks and jeans for Steve Jobs
- gray T-shirts and a hoodie for Mark Zuckerberg
- blue or grey suits for Obama (He told Vanity Fair in 2014 that he only wears blue or grey suits in order to pare down the number of trivial decisions he has to make in order to make some room for the BIG decisions his job demands that he make.)

Ultimately, making more conscious choices about what you buy, what you keep, and what you discard will significantly reduce your clutter.

Beyond clothing and stuff...be deliberate with your CHOICES

When you deliberately choose (and refusing to choose is still a choice), you are responsible for what happens. Sure, you might choose wrong. And truthfully, the thought of being wrong makes you afraid. When you are afraid, you cannot act.

Instead, get comfortable making faster decisions. For example, if you buy something, try it on again at home and decide you don't like it, don't just put it aside. Put it by the front door with the receipt so the next time you leave the house, you can return it. If you can't return it, donate it immediately. This eliminates a potential "pile" of stuff you don't want and "don't know" what to do with.

Other types of clutter that build up include emails, snail mail, photos (electronic and printed), towels, sheets, dishes, toiletries, shoes, office supplies, papers, books, electronics, and more.

By sorting, purging, and getting rid of what doesn't bring you joy, isn't useful, and certainly isn't beautiful, you can eliminate significant amounts of clutter.

The final thing worth noting is you often create clutter because you are "afraid" to get rid of something. Maybe it was a gift and the giver might get angry if they found out you didn't want their gift. Or you are afraid to get rid of something because you "might need it later." There is room in life for some of this, but again, you cannot keep it all, so you must begin to make choices about what you keep and what you let go of.

Learning how to manage your clutter and practicing making faster decisions keeps stuff from piling up.

Ways to make some room

- Reduce or limit your options.
- Be clear about the difference between "good" and "bad" choices.
- Trust yourself—you know what you like and what you don't.
- An inability to decide leads to clutter.
- Use your time wisely (it's a precious and limited commodity).
- Making decisions more often leads to faster decision-making each time.
- Be discerning (with your time, energy, money).
- Have some faith. You really do know what your priorities are!
- Prioritize and take action (stop procrastinating).
- Be exclusive. Only the best gets your attention.
- Raise the bar. There are a lot of opportunities out there. Choose wisely.
- Be ruthless. Say NO a lot in order to say YES to the important.
- Unsubscribe. This includes everything that doesn't serve you (newspapers, magazines, blogs, e-zines, and even memberships you're not using).

- Let go. Give yourself permission to not know it all, have it all, do it all, try it all, or worry about it all.
- RELAX. Make some room to do nothing every single day.

Here are some decision-making POWER QUESTIONS:
(Adapted from Greg McKeown's book *Essentialism*)

- Is this the best and highest use of my time?
- Am I investing [my time, energy, money] in the right activities?
- Am I majoring in minor activities?
- Am I distinguishing between the vital few and the trivial many?
- Which problem do I want to solve (knowing I cannot solve all of them)?
- What matters most *to me*?

(See next page for your Action Step.)

ACTION STEP

The Hanger Trick

With the "Hanger Trick," the idea is to take every single hanger in your closet and hang it backward.

Decide on a period of time to run this test (a season, six months, or even a year if your closet can hold all of your clothes).

With every hanger backward, you have the opportunity to re-hang things correctly only after you wear them.

At the end of your set time, you can quickly see which hangers are still "backward."

Any hangers that are still backward hold clothing that has clearly not been worn. Now you have "proof" of what you do and don't wear. Anything you haven't worn becomes a candidate for re-selling or giving away.

Chapter 16: People first. Technology second.

If I were honest, I'd have to say I have a mildly unhealthy addiction to doing three specific things on my smartphone: checking social media sites, taking photos of my cat, and checking the weather.

Now, remember that down in the Canyon there is NO cell service. We only had the satellite phone for emergencies. So, I admit it was a true relief during the Canyon trip to not even worry about turning my phone on (in fact, I think I left it with a few other things in the car at the motel). I only missed my phone for taking photos, and instead relied on an old digital camera. That being said, I didn't take very many pictures regardless, because I was very conscious about just being in the moment, each moment of the trip! And it was fabulous!

Beyond the Canyon

Have you seen the commercial with a dad sitting between his two daughters on a couch? The dad is looking left and right at his daughters, who are both on their phones, thumbs busily texting away. He sighs and says, "You're texting each other, aren't you?"

When I gather with people for a meal or attend an event, inevitably I see this "thing" happening. People stare at their little tiny screens and poke them with their thumbs. Other people around us stare at televisions hung on the walls.

I want to scream, "People—put down the phone. Turn off the television!"

Communication suffers. Relationships suffer.

How about we do the old-fashioned thing and *talk to* the people around us? They matter. So do you.

Are you "ON" all the time?

Catherine Steiner-Adair, a clinical and consulting psychologist at Harvard, recently wrote *The Big Disconnect: Protecting Childhood and Family Relationships in the Digital Age*. She interviewed more than 1,000 kids (ages four to eighteen). She talked to hundreds of teachers and parents. She noted that children of any age (from the very young to those who were nearly adults) were frustrated by the lack of attention their parents showed them when the parents were looking at any kind of technology and particularly when they were looking at screens (computers, tablets, smartphones).

Here's a question to ask people in your life: *Do you feel like you have to compete with my phone [tablet, computer] for my attention?*

If the answer is YES from any of them, it's time to put down the device and PAY ATTENTION.

Culture of Distraction
(Adapted from a talk by Joe Kraus: http://joekraus.com/were-creating-a-culture-of-distraction)

A question to ask yourself: *Are you happy with your relationship with your phone/tablet? Do you think it's a healthy one?*

Studies indicate we are:
- increasingly disconnected from the people and events around us
- unable to engage in long-form thinking (These days, we feel anxious when our brains are unstimulated.)
- threatening our own creativity and insight as we fill in our "gap time" with stimulation ("gap time" is a KEY ingredient for creativity and insight and can include "long-form" thinking...see above)
- devaluing real human connection when we prioritize devices (phones, tablets, laptops) over people right in front of us

I read something recently that explained people's lives were disrupted by noisy factories, trains, and cars in the early 20th century.

When the time clock was introduced into factories, it added a stressful "time" element that hadn't existed before.

Next came telephones, radio, and televisions. We still have all those things, except now we can hold them in the palms of our hands and carry them everywhere with us.

I sincerely think it was a gift to spend such a long stretch of time away from my smartphone and computer.

During our trip, there were a couple of people who checked the satellite phone daily, mostly because of family needs. Nelson made one collect call home to check in with his mom. I didn't think about it or worry about it. Rather, I found great peace in realizing the world will keep turning with or without my input.

It was also a great comfort to sit in groups and talk without being distracted by anything beyond another raft group floating by or a particularly beautiful sunset. I loved the act of connection, being deeply in conversation with people on my trip and feeling heard and being seen.

Ways to make some room

There are things you can do to deliberately put people first (and put technology second):

Go through the list below. CIRCLE IN RED the ones you (and perhaps your family) are committed to trying. Then, give it a try for a week or a month and notice how your relationships change (hopefully for the better)!

- During any meal, put away your device(s).
- When someone asks you a question, put down your device. If you're in the middle of something, let them know, finish what you're doing, and then put down your device.
- Consider "disconnecting" from technology one day a week. I know many people who take a sabbatical from social media on Sundays. Or they at least turn off their cell phones.
- I am not a fan of driving and talking on the phone for any important conversation. You cannot do two things at once and expect to do either of them well. My opinion: drive or talk on the phone. Don't do both.
- Understand that your need to "be connected" 24/7/365 has roots in FOMO. Remember you cannot know it all, read it all, keep it all, do it all, have it all, or be it all. And that's actually a good thing.

ACTION STEP

Go through the list above. CIRCLE IN RED the ones you (and perhaps your family) are committed to trying. Then, give it a try for a week or a month and notice how your relationships change (hopefully for the better)!

Chapter 17: Say the thing that's the hardest to say from a place of humility and love (you'll never be sorry).

Group dynamics being what they are, there was conflict during our river trip. For instance, we had a few issues figuring out the kitchen routine and having a qualified person act as "kitchen master."

There was some confusion over the schedule of the trip and one guy stepped up to plan out where we could potentially camp as the trip progressed. He didn't have to, but he took on the responsibility to keep us organized. I think there was a conversation that ended with him saying, "Look, I'm just going to do this because I don't see anyone else stepping up." He wasn't angry...he just wanted to have a plan (and the rest of us appreciated that).

As the trip wore on, a couple of guys didn't get along (and came nearly to fisticuffs toward the end of the trip).

I've heard worse stories from others on their river trips, including one that experienced a full-on mutiny against their leader. Thankfully, nothing on our trip was that bad.

However, being with fifteen other people for sixteen days means you either need to resolve conflicts or you stop speaking. And when there's a limited supply of people to speak to and you're all stuck together on a few rafts, things can get awkward fast.

It's best to say what needs to be said and get on with it. Pride and ego have no place on a trip like this (nor in life, for that matter).

Beyond the Canyon

I like storytelling. Not just the kind of storytelling you read in books or hear at storytelling festivals. The kind of storytelling I'm talking about happens when YOU are making up stories, either in your head or in conversation with friends. Mostly, they start like this:

- What if...?
- Why didn't...?
- How come...?
- Do you think...?

See, we often start making up stories in order to try and make sense of something. The problem is we can do this at the expense of doing the hard work.

What's the hard work?

The hard work is actually approaching the person we're telling stories about and asking him or her about their thoughts. Or we can decide not to make up a story at all and instead just asking the person straight out.

Rather than making up stories, ask the hard question. Have the difficult conversation. End the storytelling in your head and ask the person directly.

It actually takes personal leadership and integrity to ask a question. Or to gather a group when there's been conflict. Or to create a safe space for a conversation to be had (rather than letting a confrontation boil up).

Ways to make some room

Here's an easy summary for saying the thing that's hardest to say:

- If you are sorry, say so.
- If you were wrong, say so.
- If you're angry or hurt, say so.
- If you're confused, say so.
- If you're frightened, say so.
- If you think you're right, say so (but be an active listener and have a conversation...just in case you're wrong or don't know the whole story).

Engage the person in conversation instead of investing your precious time and energy creating made up stories (which can end up being so wrong).

I'm not saying this is easy. You might need to start practicing this in small ways before you embark on some of the bigger conversations.

The most helpful pieces of advice I've been given include:

- Think of the interaction as a conversation rather than a confrontation.
- Choose to be uncomfortable for the five minutes the conversation will take rather than being miserable, frustrated, or angry for the next five weeks, five months, or five years.
- Practice asking for what you need in a clear and direct manner. Practice, practice, practice.
- Go for long-term respect over short-term popularity.

ACTION STEP

Think through your current relationships. Is there something you're ready to address with another person? Arrange a time to sit down with them and speak from your heart, without needing to be "right" or to "win." Just say what needs to be said. Then really hear how the other person responds.

Chapter 18: Lie in the grass and listen to the secrets it tells you. Smile with the flowers. Hug the trees.

Deep at the bottom of the Canyon, I was literally surrounded by jaw-dropping views. It was mesmerizing to look up and see the layers and layers of canyon walls and follow them upward as my eyes rose and rose and rose, seeking each wall beyond the next.

Looking at the variety of rocks that created those mile-high walls was beyond impressive. There are layers upon layers of rock with a dizzying array of formations, types of rock, colors, and textures.

And then there's the water, which can change from green or blue to brown with a single rainstorm. The side rivers of Havasu and the Little Colorado are stained the most brilliant turquoise because of their travertine mineral content. As this water melds with the emerald green canyon water, I found myself literally breathless because of the beauty laid out in front of me. We were really grateful that no rainstorms turned our gorgeous green waters into a roiling froth of chocolate milk colored chaos.

The miracle of Grand Canyon is how she begs you to slow down and pay attention.

Twice during our trip, Nelson was visited by scorpions. The very first night, a large black one scampered across his stomach as he lay sleeping on the sand. Feeling something, he flipped his sleeping bag up with his knees. The scorpion flew in the air and landed near his head. As my husband rolled around to look at it, the scorpion reared up and made a screeching noise before Nelson grabbed his hat and flipped the insect into the bushes.

The second scorpion visitor was only discovered on the morning as Nelson was rolling up his sleeping pad. A very small, translucently yellow scorpion had managed to crawl under the pad. Nelson had no idea it was there. Was it under there all night? The group gathered around to take a look, both admiring and fearing this small, odd creature.

Daytime found many of us joining up for side hikes to explore places with magical names like "Elves Chasm" (and to jump off those moss-covered ledges into the cool, inviting pool of green water below), the grain mills high above the river at Nankoweap, and to tackle the strenuous hike up to Deer Creek (where we were treated to an incredible oasis of cool green at the top).

We also encountered (but did not touch) our Native American past as we hiked along walls decorated with pictographs from local tribes as well as signatures and company names from prospectors who lived, worked, and passed through Grand Canyon. We saw areas with huge bolts where the government considered adding additional dams for hydroelectric power, and we passed still-sacred Hopi salt mines cliffs near the water's edge.

Each day was exciting as we had the opportunity to spy great horned sheep resting and grazing along the river banks or climbing high up on the Canyon hills and walls.

And night time. Oh, night time! As the sun began to set each evening, the heat would lift off our shoulders like a heavy, wool blanket we'd toss aside. The colors would wow us to the point where we'd stop our activity to just stare; we were powerless to do anything beyond gazing at the colors while breathing in the cooler evening air. As night descended, the stars made their entrance as a brilliant, twinkling white quilt over our heads. We were dazzled by the sight of it.

Despite not wearing a watch and never knowing the time, I seemed to wake up each night around the same time. I'd wake up, slip on my glasses, and gaze at the Milky Way stretching across the sky. It was like a divine art show painted each night just for me.

And every morning just before the sun would rise, I would open my eyes, slip on my glasses, and see the bats overhead swooping and whirling as they caught their morning's breakfast of gnats and flies and other winged bugs.

The point of my rhapsodic musings here? I was fully attuned to my surroundings. I was gobsmacked by the gifts and beauty of nature. I was connected deeply to the environment I was in. To me, these things are the point of being ALIVE.

Beyond the Canyon

Outside of my Grand Canyon experience, I find myself deeply in love with, and in awe of, nature. I will run outside to see a gorgeous sunset. I will stop and marvel at a brilliant rainbow. You will see me run around in the snow just feel the flakes on my face. I've been known to love sleeping in a tent out in a rainstorm.

Another immediate and easy way for me to connect with nature is through gardening. In fact, it's a bit of a moving meditation for me. There's something relaxing and very grounding for me pulling weeds, planting seeds, and nurturing something to grow.

Nature is healing for my spirit. Spending time each day lying in the grass and basking in the sun can be incredibly restorative (and a great source of Vitamin D). As a little girl, I used to wrap myself in a blanket and sit outside on our covered porch just to watch it rain.

I discovered a deeper love of nature while rafting the American River, camping each summer with my family in California, always wanting to ride horses, discovering hiking as a teenager, and learning to backpack and kayak in my late 20s.

Nature is my happy place, where I go to recharge, relax, and rejuvenate.

Ways to make some room

Here's a fascinating way for YOU to begin cultivating a new, deeper relationship with nature.

"Forest bathing" (also known as "Shinrin-yoku") was developed in Japan in the 1980s. This meditative walking activity that asks you to consciously and deliberately engage with nature using all five of your senses:

1. Sight
2. Sound
3. Taste
4. Touch
5. Smell

I'm just crazy enough to also engage a sixth sense—my intuition and perception. To *feel* into the place I'm in.

With forest bathing, your walk is to be done in silence—no buddies, no personal electronic devices, etc.

You're asked to tune in to what sparks your senses, like the texture of birch bark or the scent of wild flowers or pinecones. Bend down and feel the moss. Find a seat, get quiet and watch what happens in the forest when you are still.

Here's the basic idea during your walk:

- breathe

- relax
- wander
- touch
- listen
- heal

Appreciating nature for her silence, beauty, colors, and for how she changes through the seasons is an excellent habit to practice daily. The more you notice nature, the more she nurtures you. The more important she will (hopefully) become.

And when something is important, you'll work to protect it. And in protecting it, you protect all of us (the animals, people, and even the plants) long term, too.

One easy way to notice nature is to just go outside and sit. Watch the wind move the trees and leaves. See how the bugs wander, but with purpose.

And I'm fond of saying, "Just take time to watch the birdies do their birdie thing."

This combination of mindfulness and time spent in nature are immersive healing activities.

Here's the BEST secret: most of my Grand Canyon group practiced Shinrin-Yoku without even knowing they were doing it.

ACTION STEP

Schedule a Shinrin-yoku adventure! Deliberately engage with nature using all six of your senses:

1. Sight
2. Sound
3. Taste
4. Touch
5. Smell
6. Feel (internal)

Tune in to what sparks your senses, like the texture of tree bark or the scent of wild flowers or sight of curvaceous pinecones. Bend down and feel the moss. Find a seat, get quiet and watch what happens in the forest when you are still.

Photo courtesy of Jenni Miehle

Chapter 19: Love is all there is.

Albert Einstein noted we have one important decision to make: whether we believe the universe is a friendly or a hostile place.

Life isn't us vs. them.

Life is only WE.

Be present with people. Have compassion for them (and for yourself).

Forget about accomplishments, accolades, or even knowing the "right" people. Life is about relationships, community, and spiritual connection. It's about being present with the people you're with. It's about treading lightly on the earth and using the Earth's resources wisely.

On overcoming fear

If you haven't realized it yet, much of this book teaches you how to deal with fear: the fear of not being enough, not doing enough, not having enough (or having too much); a fear of remembering, forgetting, or even offending. And there's the fear of DOING.

Our modern society makes us afraid—of ourselves, of each other, and even of our natural world. Most everything you hear on TV is fear-based. A lot of what you read in popular media encourages you to be better, make more money, buy into convenience, protect what's yours, or get what's due to you.

Instead of fear, I want to talk about love and the concept of "enough."

I don't want to talk about romantic love or co-dependent love, or even parental or familial love.

I want to talk about unconditional love. Love that has no expectations. Love that allows each of us to be who we are. The kind of love that allows who we are to be enough.

In his book *True Love*, Buddhist monk Thich Nhat Hanh says, "You must love in such a way that the person you love feels free."

It's taken me a long time to realize my love came with strings attached. Often I loved in order to "get" something from someone else (like security, love, significance or control).

Very recently, I realized that love of myself came with conditions, too. If I ate right, I was "good" and lovable. If I didn't piss people off, I was okay. And if I didn't ever do things wrong (hello, Type A, Perfectionist Angie), then I was worthy of being loved by myself and others.

Now, I realize something profound: we are all worthy of giving and receiving love simply because we are alive.

Ways to make some room

Grand Canyon is a place that demands respect. And because of that, I love and honor her water, her creatures, and even her rocks and dirt.

Grand Canyon does not question who she is; she just is. And that is enough.

I sincerely believe that we—each of us—also just are. And that is enough. And because of that, we are worthy of love and respect.

ACTION STEP

Practice loving kindness in everything you do. Infuse it into your being—it's truly who you are. I sincerely believe LOVE IS ALL THERE IS and it is your natural state of being.

Practice loving everyone (your friends and "enemies") with wild abandon. See how this practice enriches and changes your life for the better.

Who you are right now is enough. Share love. Practice love. Each of us is enough and worthy of love right now. Share it.

Chapter 20: Slow down. Breathe. Make some damn room!

The gift of a sixteen-day, 225-mile rafting trip through one of the most remote places in the United States is the gift of having some room.

- Room to breathe.
- Room to talk.
- Room to be silent.
- Room to be alone.

This gift of time also allowed Nelson and me to have long conversations about what we liked about our life and about what we'd like to change.

Very shortly after our trip, we changed everything. Nelson finished remodeling our house. We decided to rent out that house in that town we didn't love and move to the mountains (which we very much love). We packed up our lives and both our businesses. Shortly after that, we got married. A year after that, we sold 80 percent of what we owned and moved into a 280-square foot fifth wheel camper. Now we're on the verge of starting a new business together, continuing to plan epic outdoor adventures, and loving our lives.

All this happened because we slowed down. We made some room...and it just happened to be sixteen days and 225 miles long.

Beyond the Canyon

I've sat with more people than I can count and listened to them rattle off their to dos, volunteer commitments, and kids' school and activities schedules.

It makes me exhausted sometimes realizing how over-scheduled some people have made their lives.

And often when I go into people's homes and offices, I am overwhelmed by the amount of STUFF they have.

That makes me extra exhausted.

The daily life clutter, the physical clutter, the mental clutter, and even the emotional clutter make me want to shout, "IT'S ALL TOO MUCH!"

Here's the thing...we're so busy reacting to life as it comes speeding toward us that we have no time to respond thoughtfully.

Unless…

Unless we take a pause long enough to *realize* this is happening.

Unless someone opens our eyes to a different way.

If you haven't realized how overcommitted, overscheduled, and over it you are yet, I want to be the one who opens your eyes to it.

I feel your overwhelm.

I feel your exhaustion. I felt your panic. I feel your resignation.

I felt my own overwhelm, my own exhaustion, panic, and resignation.

The truth is I think I've always known I wanted something different for my life.

And the longer I'm in business for myself, the more I realize how I need more and more downtime, with longer stretches of rest.

The longer I work with clients in my business, the more I realize *they* also need those same things.

So, gentle reader, I applaud you for having made it to this point of the book. Here's a vitally important question:

Where can you make some room in YOUR life?

Ways to make some room

In order to figure out how to make some room in your life, start here:

- Where are you feeling exhausted?
- What feels like a heavy obligation?
- Where are you overcommitted, overstuffed, uncomfortable, or overwhelmed?
- Are you running out of room for all the stuff in your home, office, or anywhere else?
- Do you find yourself holding your breath because of stress?
- Is your posture locked stiffly into place?
- Do you find new aches, pains, pops, and cracks in your body each day?
- Do you suffer with a chronic illness?
- Do you feel disconnected from your family?
- Are you starving for true nourishment and real food?
- Are you lonely?
- Is there a dream inside you that you've stuffed way, way down because if feels unreachable, impractical, or just plain silly?

I want you to know you can have what you want. Good health. A sane schedule. Real community. Living your dreams.

It IS possible.

Here's how you begin: slow down. Then take some deep breaths. Start to make some room for what matters to you most.

I won't say it's easy, or that it will be done fast, but it can be done.

I dare you to try it.

ACTION STEP

Slow down.

Breathe.

Make some room.

Threats to the Colorado River and Grand Canyon

Chapter Contributed by: River Runners For Wilderness (https://rrfw.org/)

You may think Grand Canyon is just the National Park.

Most people do, until they look at a map.

A quick glance at a map clearly shows that the geographical Grand Canyon goes from a place called Lee's Ferry in the east, 280 river miles to the Grand Wash Cliffs in the west. The Grand Wash Cliffs define the western edge of the Colorado Plateau. The northern and southern rim escarpments are the north and south boundaries.

Going forward, let's refer to the entire Grand Canyon as THE Grand Canyon.

As such, there are a number of agencies and first nations with an actual presence in THE Grand Canyon. There is Grand Canyon National Park (GRCA), the Bureau of Land Management (BLM), the United States Forest Service, the Navajo Nation (NN), Hualapai Nation and Havasupai Nation. The Hopi Nation, with an actual reservation some seventy miles to the east of THE Grand Canyon, have clear religious connections to specific locations in the Grand Canyon, as do the Zuni Nation and Southern Piute Nation.

All told, there's:

1. the geographical place
2. a handful of groups with management control of an actual part of THE Grand Canyon

Let's look at some of the current developments or plans for developments in THE Grand Canyon and the environmental concerns that accompany these developments.

1. A commercialized river runs through it.

River running in Grand Canyon surely occurred before historic times, especially when the river was warm and running with little water in the fall of most years. Ample driftwood logs would have made good material for crude rafts held together with yucca fiber ropes.

Between 1869, when the first documented river runners traveled through Grand Canyon, and the end of 1949, only 100 river runners had traveled all the way through THE Grand Canyon, from Lee's Ferry to the Grand Wash Cliffs.

In 1955, GRCA implemented a permit system for river runners. It was a simple process back then. Fill out a one page form and go. Except the NPS would not award permits to anyone who had not been through THE Grand Canyon by boat.

This simple requirement to get a permit allowed commercial river companies to ask for and receive permit after permit, while do-it-yourself river runners who had not traveled through Grand Canyon were turned away. Even if the DIY folks were world champion kayakers or were experienced on other rivers, they were denied a permit if they had no Grand Canyon experience.

Commercial river running greatly increased under this management, and the NPS finally froze all increases in river use in 1972, when there were very few DIY river runners and the majority of river trips (over 90 percent) were commercial trips. Even today, in the middle of the busy summer season, the DIY river runners will launch one trip to the commercial companies' four launches.

Once established as river concessionaires by the National Parks Service, these same businesses lobbied successfully to halt the passage of a Wilderness Management Plan for Grand Canyon National Park. To this day, while GRCA is 97 percent wilderness, the park has no congressionally designated wilderness.

2. **Various groups want to build a tramway, hotel, shopping mall, and trailer park on the rim of Grand Canyon.**

A Phoenix-based group of developers plans to have up to 10,000 people a day ride a tramway from the rim of Grand Canyon 4,000 feet down to the Colorado River. There are huge issues surrounding this plan. They include:

- Restroom facilities. There will be a bathroom built at the bottom of the tram able to service 10,000 people a day, built next to one of the last spawning grounds of the threatened Humpback Chub, a native fish.
- Trash facilities. On the rim at the top of the tramway, there is no landfill. In fact, there is no trash service at all.
- Lack of water. There is also no water in this area of high desert. Read more to about the water issues in the Southwest to learn why this is such a monumental issue.
- "Natural Quiet" and "Dark Skies" as important natural resources (that are becoming valuable commodities). Part of the tramway development includes an airport and heliport at the bottom of the tramway. Constant air tour noise would destroy wildlife habitat for miles around. Besides the visual and auditory scar a development like this would produce, the nighttime light pollution would be visible for miles in every direction.
- Sacred Lands. The Hopi Nation considers the Tramway area sacred land. Any development there would adversely impact their cultural heritage. Another group opposed to this development are the local Navajo who have been grazing animals in these areas since time immemorial. These local Navajo do not want a mega-resort in their traditional sacred homeland.

3. Increased helicopter operations at the bottom of THE western Grand Canyon on Hualapai land near the Grand Canyon Skywalk has made this the busiest heliport on the planet.

This development has destroyed the "Natural Quiet" soundscape in what is the most remote wilderness landscape in the entire USA outside of Alaska. The native Big Horn Sheep are no longer seen in this area due to the incessant helicopter noise.

4. Uranium mining on both the North and South Rims just back of the rim escarpments on BLM and USFS land threatens this sensitive ecosystem.

Uranium is highly toxic and stays toxic for a long, long time (think: tens of thousands of years). Given that the Colorado River is the drinking water source for Las Vegas, Phoenix, Tucson, and San Diego, a radioactive spill of any type could adversely impact the drinking water for tens of millions of people. Once the minerals are extracted, the cleanup of these toxic mines typically falls on the shoulders of the US taxpayers, in the form of superfund cleanups.

5. Growth of the gateway community of Tusayan will affect water, public utilities, and the natural surroundings due to an increase in population and traffic.

Tusayan is a tiny town (population less than 600) located near the South Rim of the Grand Canyon. There is enormous controversy surrounding this town regarding proposed future expansion and development. Water issues, population density, and degradation of the "Natural Quiet" and "Dark Sky" parks all come into play here.

Think of THE Grand Canyon as a big mountain with a large river slicing through it. That mountain is in the middle of an even bigger desert. There is not a lot of water around it. Flagstaff, Arizona, located seventy miles south of THE Grand Canyon, gets its water from wells that are over 3,000 feet deep. When a developer announces a new building project, they are required to define where the water will come from. Additionally, the need to address transportation, jobs, and more are crucial to any new developments surrounding THE Grand Canyon.

6. While having no presence on the ground, there is an ever-increasing amount of tourist-based helicopter and fixed-wing aircraft overflights in the skies over THE Grand Canyon.

We have covered this ground already talking about the need to preserve "Natural Quiet" as a resource. There are parts of the park where aircraft noise is incessant all day due to tour flights and much of the night with all the high-flying commercial jetliners going in and out of Las Vegas and the Los Angeles basin further west.

7. Glen Canyon Dam is a mere 13 miles upriver from Lee's Ferry.

Built in the 1950s, this Dam just celebrated its fiftieth year of water control of the Colorado River in THE Grand Canyon. A Frankenstorm in the upper basin of the Colorado River could destroy this dam (and will one day), causing huge ecological damage to the river corridor through THE Grand Canyon.

The construction of Glen Canyon Dam has radically altered the Colorado River in Grand Canyon. You most likely know Colorado is Spanish for red. The Colorado River is a steep river carving into soft sea sediments aging from fifty to 500 million years old. The Dam has made a reservoir behind it that has captured almost all the silt that would normally head through THE Grand Canyon on the way to the Sea of Cortez. The local native fish, like the Chub, are blind. They need no eyes in water so muddy that it's pitch dark three inches under the water's surface.

Before the dam, as the river chewed at its banks, big trees would get undercut and wash into the river and float on through, only to get trapped in huge driftwood piles. This driftwood supplies nutrients for small insects the fish eat. When a dam is built (like Glen Canyon), the silt flow is blocked. The result is blind fish then get eaten by fish that can see (like imported trout, considered a "sport" fish), trees no longer fall into the river to act as driftwood for bugs to eat, their habit is destroyed, and fish no longer have bugs to eat.

Let's also talk temperature. Before the dam, the Colorado River would freeze over in the winter and heat up to over 70 degrees in the summer. The native fish grew up used to this swing. Now the water comes out at the bottom of the dam at about 55 degrees, too cold for good fish sex and raising young fish. The result is that the non-native fish, like the trout that are clear water sight feeders and do better in colder water, are out-competing the native fish.

8. Finally, as America has been managing THE Grand Canyon since the late 1800s, the population of the Southwestern United States has seen the biggest migration in the history of our species to the region around Grand Canyon.

A huge increase in population has occurred at Las Vegas to the west, Salt Lake City to the north, Albuquerque to the east, and Phoenix/Tucson to the south. With the advent of the internet, the sensitive archeological sites, seeps and springs, and the backcountry in general of THE Grand Canyon have seen increase foot and All-Terrain Vehicle (ATV) impacts.

2015 was a perfect storm for the National Park Service at Grand Canyon National Park (GRCA). The government sequestration cut back funding for staffing at GRCA just when gasoline prices dropped and America hit the road for a vacation to...our national parks, of course. GRCA resources were put into cleaning the bathrooms and law enforcement, while the park's own Science Center saw continued staffing cuts. Who will be monitoring the resource for damage by too many visitors if all staff are in janitorial maintenance and enforcement?

Visitors pay an entrance fee. Some (not all) of the proceeds from gate fees go to staffing in the park. If the funding from Washington dries up, then local gate funding sources become more important. So the agency has to turn a blind eye to the damage that is happening to the resource by too much visitation just so they can realize increased revenue from more gate fees. It is a vicious cycle that adversely impacts the resource with the construction of more parking lots (pave paradise to put up a parking lot). The need for GRCA to make more money off of visitors has direct impact on planning for backcountry use levels.

The last river management plan greatly increased DIY river running in the off season. GRCA collects $100 from every DIY river runner. More river runners equals more money to operate the park. It is a slippery slope that causes the park to allow increased crowding. We lose the very things that attracted us to these resources in the first place: solitude and a primitive and unconfined type of experience.

Solitude and a primitive and unconfined type of experience was what the First Nation people saw when they arrived in small groups on the North American continent. That type of experience is exactly what GRCA is to manage for, especially in the wilderness backcountry. Simple pressure from more people to experience THE Grand Canyon is changing what the very experience will be. Meanwhile, outside the GRCA managed lands, we see increased ATV traffic, helicopter tours, tramway construction plans, and mining and hunting pressure. These activities adversely impact the very ecology of The Canyon in ways we are just barely beginning to understand.

Beyond the Canyon

Those pressures being felt around THE Grand Canyon are the same pressures being experienced all across the United States and beyond.

Our outdoor spaces, our water resources, and our natural heritage is being "loved to death."

What can you, as one single person, do?

It's simple really. In order to support THE Grand Canyon and other National and State parks, and to preserve/conserve natural lands and water anywhere, start in your own community.

Ask your friends to help you identify who is doing clean-ups of local waterways in your town. Get involved.

If you can, help fund local grassroots non-profits (like River Runners for Wilderness) that are doing work to protect our waterways, lands, and parks.

Give your time, your energy, and yes, even your money. It's needed...YOU'RE needed.

The land and water thank you for your support.

ACTION STEP

1. Support River Runners for Wilderness and the good work they are doing for the Colorado River and Grand Canyon. Donate here: https://rrfw.org/

AND/OR

2. Find a cause in your backyard that matters deeply to you. Support the "Friends of" and "Riverkeepers" groups. A simple web search will lead you to them.

Action Step Roundup

Chapter 1: Your brain is not for remembering.

Think of one repetitive thing you do daily or weekly. Sit down and create a checklist for it. Be it business or personal, your brain will thank you for it!

Chapter 2: It is easier to keep up than to catch up.

Create a routine for anything:

1. Decide what needs to be done.
2. Commit to it (daily, weekly, monthly, yearly).
3. Gather the supplies you need (if any).
4. Carve out and dedicate the time (even if it is just two minutes once a day).
5. Do the thing.
6. Then give yourself a Big High-Five!

Chapter 3: Two minutes now saves hours later.

Jump on those two-minute wins! Here are some examples to get you started:

- Put your phone, wallet, and keys in the same place every day.
- Prep first (then cook).
- File, shred, trash.
- Exercise and stretch.
- Return a hard call or email instead of avoiding it.

- Say the thing that's hard to say.
- Brush and floss.
- Breathe purposefully.
- Refill your subscription or prescription before you are out.
- Go ahead and buy the big pack of toilet paper.
- Double check the tie-downs on the kayaks on top of your car (just sayin').
- Keep up with your continuing education, expiration dates on your web hosting, and more.

Chapter 4: Getting organized is work. Staying organized is habit.

Here are two examples of daily routines you could adopt. Adapt them for yourself. Remember: SIMPLICITY is KEY.

Morning
- meditation
- exercise/yoga
- sitting still while enjoying a cup of coffee or tea
- writing or journaling
- preparing for the day and week

Evening
- tidying your office before you leave
- creating a to-do list for your next day
- meditation
- exercise
- savoring a meal with friends or family
- taking a hot bath
- writing or journaling

Chapter 5: Take the time, get quiet, feel into it. Immerse yourself.

Rest, Play, Be Wild

Go and do whatever it is that makes you smile, feel like a kid, connects you with your spirit, gets your hands dirty, covers you with paint and glitter, and makes your stomach hurt from laughing.

This could be anything from sitting quietly watching the birds and chipmunks do their thing to dancing naked in the backyard while running through the sprinklers.

It's completely your choice. Do what makes you HAPPY.

Chapter 6: Be discerning about where you spend your energy (reading, doing, watching, eating).

Answer these questions and you'll be much farther along the path of satisfaction and happiness. You'll avoid procrastination. And you'll end your overwhelm.

1. What IS the best and highest use of my time?
2. What are my God-given gifts and talents?
3. What do I love doing?
4. What can I STOP doing?

Chapter 7: Be bold. Be brave. Take action. (Even if you're scared shitless while doing it.)

Learning to manage your breath is the key to life. Breathe from your chest and moving down into your abdomen. Pooch your stomach out! In fact, think of your abdomen like a ball—as you breathe, you want to fill that ball with air. Then slowly release.

After a few deep breaths, move into deliberate breathing. Breathe in for five seconds, concentrating on the air moving into your nostrils, into your chest, and down into your belly. Then reverse. Concentrate on moving the air through your nose as you empty your belly and chest. Repeat slowly.

Chapter 8: Laugh often and loudly.

Choose that thing about yourself that bugs you. Spend some time with it. Go through this exercise again.
If you've lived in shame of this "thing" of yours, now's the time to begin discovering how to embrace it.

By eliminating your hatred, fear, and loathing of this "thing" that is part of you, you are making some room for love, acceptance, and tolerance for yourself.

Grab a pen and start writing:

My thing is:_____

The negative emotions I feel about it are:

_____

_____

_____

The positive emotions I want to feel about it are:

_____

_____

_____

Next, see how you can begin to catch yourself each time you begin to think that negative thought. Go back to your list and choose a more positive thought. Practice thinking and/or saying that positive thing out loud.

Choose a friend and do this exercise together. See how you can support each other in accepting these weird, odd, and kooky things about yourselves!

Chapter 9: Reclaim your nights and weekends. #UNPLUG

Simple: #UNPLUG
Try it for an evening or even for an entire weekend.

Chapter 10: Busy is a bullshit word. Stop saying it. Choose to say something real.

Banish "busy" from your vocabulary. It will change how you feel about your life. And it can create the opportunity for deeper conversation and connection between you and the person/people you're with.

Chapter 11: Keep only the useful, beautiful, and joyful.

Go through the list below and CIRCLE IN RED the ones you're committed to simplifying in your life. Then, pull out your calendar and schedule one hour (each day, each week, or each month) to purge each area you circled.

- What's on your desk? Visual clutter is so distracting!
- Declutter your space—less to dust, less to clean.
- Get stuff OFF your to-do list—you're not getting to a lot of it anyway, right?
- Clear out your brain—hello, Monkey Mind! (You know, the endless chatter that fills our heads, drowns our hearts, and starves our souls.)
- Reduce your clothes, shoes, accessories—fewer choices means fewer decisions. Keeping only what you LOVE and WEAR simplifies your mornings. Yes, this means you'll wear your clothes more often—people will see you in the same clothes a lot. So?
- Declutter your morning and evening routines—start your day calmly and with conscious choices. End your day with stillness and connection to yourself and your family.
- Get rid of books, CDs, DVDs and even that old record collection. Keep only what you use and love. Everything else is you living in the past or worrying about the future. Be here now—keep what you use now.
- Clients, customers, projects—yes, fire them if they are a pain in the ass, abusive to you or your staff, aren't bringing you satisfaction, or if they aren't making you money (and especially if they are making you LOTS of money but are one of the first three things I mentioned). Pain in the ass clients who are disrespectful, mean, late for appointments, late to pay, etc. ARE NOT WORTH THE ENERGY OR TIME OR MONEY. You're kidding

yourself if you think they are (especially if it's about money).

- Get rid of PAPER! Seriously, when was the last time you looked at half of what you're keeping? Unless you need it for legal or tax reasons or you're actively using it for a project, get rid of it!
- Reduce the sentimental stuff. If it's sentimental (photos, books, kids artwork) do you need to keep it all? Can you pare it down to a few treasured pieces? Can you digitize any of it? Remember—it isn't about the "thing" it's about the emotion the "thing" makes you FEEL.
- Throw out or donate food you won't/can't/should not be eating. Past the expiration? Toss it. Didn't like it? Donate it. It's crap? Throw it away (or if unopened and you have the receipt, return it).
- Cleaning products are clutter. Often we just have too much. And [rant alert] most of these products are poisons. You can do A LOT with baking soda, vinegar, and essential oils.
- Art—does it still bring you joy? If it doesn't sell it, donate it, or give it away. Just because it used be "awesome" doesn't mean you're stuck with it for life!
- Stuff related to hobbies—are you still actively participating! Great—keep what you use and get rid of the rest. Not doing the hobby anymore? You're living in the past—time to bless it, release it, and free up the space (mentally and physically) for something NEW.
- Office supplies—when the sticky notes are so old the sticky is gone, it's time to start throwing stuff away! Envelopes, business cards, pens, pencils, office machines, dried up white out, rubber bands

that are dry and rotted, old folders...the list goes on.

Chapter 12: We cannot know it all, read it all, keep it all, do it all, have it all, or be it all. And that's actually a good thing.

What activities can you purposefully and thoughtfully remove from your to-do list? Review the list below for ideas:

- people pleasing
- obsessively checking email over and over and over
- multi-tasking
- saying "yes" to everything, always without thought
- reacting to all messages (email, voicemail, text, snail mail)
- doing it all
- not getting enough sleep, exercise, sex
- perfectionism ("Shitty first drafts" are awesome! Thanks, Anne Lamott.)
- skipping meals
- not taking time to pee, stretch, or otherwise get away from your desk during the day
- getting bogged down needing to know it all before starting
- getting stuck because you don't know "how"
- holding your breath (here's a secret: breath is LIFE)
- procrastinating (UNLESS it's part of your process)
- doing all the little "safe" stuff before tackling the big "risky" stuff
- apologizing (ladies—this might be for you)

- fitting in "one more thing" before heading out the door
- ignoring your Soul's calling
- hiding, shrinking
- boasting, faking
- doing laundry instead of your "Right Work"
- staring at your phone instead of being present with the person in front of you
- avoiding the difficult conversations (tip: five seconds of discomfort now instead of five days or weeks or months of resentment later)

Chapter 13: Kill your microwave. Throw out your TV.

Go through the list below. CIRCLE IN RED the ones you (and perhaps your family) are committed to trying. Then, give it a try for a week or a month and see what changes.

- Begin deliberately reducing the amount of time you watch television. An hour or two a day adds up.
- Reduce the number of shows you watch to only the ones you love and that make you feel good.
- When you're feeling really brave and have the family on board, get rid of all but one TV in the house.
- Schedule TV-free days (or weeks or months).
- Cancel your cable or satellite.
- Consider streaming services for shows you do want to watch (this will save you oodles of money).
- When you're really ready to commit, ditch all the TVs.

- Again, focus on activities that don't revolve around watching television. There are too many to list here!

Chapter 14: Stop being a mindless consumer (of information, products, and food). Start caring where "it" comes from.

Go through the list below. CIRCLE IN RED the ones you (and perhaps your family) are committed to trying. Then, give it a try for a week or a month and watch how those changes become habits!

- Compost your kitchen waste (including egg shells, coffee grounds, tea bags, and fruit and vegetable waste).
- Recycle your mixed paper, glass, and plastic.
- Recycle your aluminum and steel cans.
- Use your curbside drop off! 86 percent (approximately 254 million) of Americans have access to curbside or drop-off paper recycling programs (earth911.org). Are you participating in your recycling program? And if you don't have one, are you separating your recyclables anyway and carting them to your nearest recycling center? Sure, it's more of an effort, but it's worth it in the long run!
- When buying in bulk, bring your own re-usable mesh bags instead of using the plastic bags provided.
- Shop local (for example, at your local farmer's market). You reduce the carbon footprint of the

food you eat and reduce your exposure to pesticides. Plus, your money stays in the local economy.

- Stop buying bottled water. Bring your own refillable water bottle to the office and to special events. Get your own reusable coffee mug, too!
- Use low-flow toilets and install low-flow showerheads. Turn the tap off as you brush your teeth.
- Buy local—instead of shipping vegetables and fruits across the country (which are water-hogs to grow), buy what's local and in season. You'll help your local economy, support the small farmers, and probably eat healthier, too.
- The biggest water saver? Stop eating beef. Seriously. Watch the fantastic documentary *Cowspiracy* to learn more.

Chapter 15: Clutter is the inability (or unwillingness) to make a decision. DECIDE.

Try the Hanger Trick: the idea is to take every single hanger in your closet and hang it backward.

Decide on a period of time to run this test (a season, six months, or even a year if your closet can hold all of your clothes).

With every hanger backward, you have the opportunity to re-hang things correctly *only after you wear them.*

At the end of your set time, you can quickly see which hangers are still "backward."

Any hangers that are still backward hold clothing that has clearly not been worn. Now you have "proof" of what you do and don't wear. Anything you haven't worn becomes a candidate for re-selling or giving away.

Chapter 16: People first. Technology second.

Go through the list below. CIRCLE IN RED the ones you (and perhaps your family) are committed to trying. Then, give it a try for a week or a month and notice how your relationships change (hopefully for the better)!

- During any meal, put away your device(s).
- When someone asks you a question, put down your device. If you're in the middle of something, let them know, finish what you're doing, and then put down your device.
- Consider "disconnecting" from technology one day a week. I know many people who take a sabbatical from social media on Sundays. Or they at least turn off their cell phones.
- I am not a fan of driving and talking on the phone for any important conversation. You cannot do two things at once and expect to do either of them well. My opinion: drive or talk on the phone. Don't do both.
- Understand that your need to "be connected" 24/7/365 has roots in FOMO. Remember you cannot know it all, read it all, keep it all, do it all,

have it all, or be it all. And that's actually a good thing.

Chapter 17: Say the thing that's the hardest to say from a place of humility and love (you'll never be sorry).

Think through your current relationships. Is there something you're ready to address with another person? Arrange a time to sit down with them and speak from your heart, without needing to be "right" or to "win." Just say what needs to be said. Then really hear how the other person responds.

Chapter 18: Lie in the grass and listen to the secrets it tells you. Smile with the flowers. Hug the trees.

Schedule a Shinrin-yoku adventure! Deliberately engage with nature using all six of your senses:

1. Sight
2. Sound
3. Taste
4. Touch
5. Smell
6. Feeling (internal)

Tune in to what sparks your senses, like the texture of tree bark or the scent of wild flowers or the sight of curvaceous pinecones. Bend down and feel the moss. Find a seat, get quiet and watch what happens in the forest when you are still.

Chapter 19: Love is all there is.

Practice loving kindness in everything you do. Infuse it into your being—it's truly who you are. I sincerely believe LOVE IS ALL THERE IS and it is your natural state of being.

Practice loving everyone (your friends and "enemies") with wild abandon. See how this practice enriches and changes your life for the better.

Who you are right now is enough. Share love. Practice love. Each of us is enough and worthy of love right now. Share it.

Chapter 20: Slow down. Breathe. Make some damn room!

Slow down.
Breathe.
Make some room.

Threats to the Colorado River and Grand Canyon

1. Support River Runners for Wilderness and the good work they are doing for the Colorado River and Grand Canyon. Donate here: https://rrfw.org/

AND/OR

2. Find a cause in your backyard that matters deeply to you. Support the "Friends of" and "Riverkeepers" groups. A simple web search will lead you to them.

Epilogue

Spending sixteen days rafting Grand Canyon is the best of both worlds—we followed the current while fulfilling our dreams.

I believe we create our own reality here on earth. If there's something you're longing to do, please—go do it! Don't wait until the weekend. Don't wait for retirement. Go now. Go.

I hope the twenty ideas in the *Make Some Room Manifesto* will help you breathe deeply, make some room, and be present in your life. While I'm quite sure there are plenty of other ways you can accomplish these ideas, I simply wanted to share mine with the hope that they would help you on your happiness journey. It's a beautiful planet out there filled with beautiful people. Go out and live life! Go!

After our Grand Canyon trip, my husband and I changed EVERYTHING:

- We completed the remodel on our house and put it up for sale.
- When it didn't sell, we found a renter.
- We moved to the mountains (a place we both wanted to live).
- We re-started both our businesses in this new town.
- We got involved with a community of like-minded people, including bicyclers, climbers, hikers, beer/cider drinkers, farmers, and small business owners.
- In March of 2015, we sold most of our stuff and moved into a 30-foot fifth wheel camper with our two dogs and cat.
- In June of 2016, we paddled all 149 miles of the French Broad River (something only a few other people have done in one single trip).

We have a laundry list of adventures coming up. Too many to list here. BUT you can follow our adventures on Facebook (search for YukonandBean) or follow us on our blog at www.YukonandBean.com.

Gentle reader: Grand Canyon inspired my husband and me to follow our dreams.

How will YOU follow YOURS?

Please be Kind—Review this Book

Thanks for purchasing this book. If you enjoyed it and found the contents useful, please leave a review on Amazon! The more feedback I get from readers like you, the better future versions and titles will be. Seriously, feel free to email me at angie@yourorganizedguide.com. Your feedback matters!

ACKNOWLEDGEMENTS

I want to sincerely thank my beta-readers for their help in re-working my "shitty first draft." Big thanks to Jim and Brenda Mattson, Brooks Haislip, Marsha Cayton, Christy Macchione, Ashley Feit, Jenni Miehle (and for the creation of the *Make Some Room Manifesto* visual), and my hubby Nelson Stegall. Your suggestions, corrections, insights, and questions were invaluable!

I also have to thank Brian Aubin and Jenni Miehle for inviting Nelson and me to join this Grand Canyon trip. Without you two, this story would have never happened. Many, many thanks to you both!

About the Author

Angie Mattson Stegall is an award-winning author, executive coach/consultant, and freedom finder.

"I support leaders who are ready to ask BIG questions, to explore new perspectives, and to think outside the boring box."

Her profound sense of adventure, creativity, and her deep knowledge of "soft skills" (think: communication, emotional intelligence, diplomacy, and working with teams) allows her to guide her clients and their teams through activities in a way that invites them to engage with their own creativity. The result is individuals and teams who get excited about out-of-the-box thinking that leads to new ideas and new perspectives on their personal or professional projects, in their work, and in deeper ways that positively impacts many areas of their personal lives, too.

At this deeper level, Angie's work is grounded in love and comes from a deep place of wanting to be of service. She often says, "It's okay to want what you want. Admit what you want and want it with your whole heart." Her work is about healing. Bringing the light. Ending suffering in the world in the weird, awkward, powerful, soul-satisfying way that she does it.

Professionally, Angie teaches business and creativity seminars at community colleges based on her books and speaks to a variety of business and leadership groups. She has also been interviewed by The New York Times and NPR/WFAE's *Charlotte Talks with Mike Collins* and was the featured entrepreneur on WTVI/CPCC TV's *Great Ideas* program.

Angie won the 2014 Women's Business Award (author category) at the fifth annual Women's Business Conference and is a Founding Member of the Brevard Authors Guild.

Personally, she's an avid flatwater kayaker, hiker, and camper. She and her husband "live tiny" in Pisgah Forest, North Carolina. They explore the world under the moniker "Yukon & Bean" (www.YukonandBean.com). If you are interested in partnering, sponsoring, or inviting them to speak to your group, please reach out to yukonandbean@gmail.com.

Speaking, Workshops, Retreats:
If you're interested in working with Angie or having her speak to your group on "Making Some Room," please feel free to contact her directly at *angie@yourorganizedguide.com* or fill out the "Contact" form on her website at: www.AngieStegall.com.

Connect with Angie Mattson Stegall online

Facebook www.facebook.com/YourOrganizedGuide
LinkedIn: https://www.linkedin.com/in/angelamattsonstegall
Twitter @angiemstegall
Websites
www.AngieStegall.com and www.YukonandBean.com

(A Reminder about those freebies!)

1. FREE *Make Some Room Manifesto* Postcard

I have created a lovely full-color *Make Some Room Manifesto* postcard.

If you'd like your very own copy, simply email angie@yourorganizedguide.com with your first and last name and your full mailing address. I'll mail you a full-color postcard pronto!

---

2. Grand Canyon Photo Slide Show Online

Due to the cost of printing in full color, I've chosen to print the photos and Manifesto in black & white in this book.

However, both the Manifesto and the photos are worth viewing in COLOR.

You can grab a full-color copy of the Manifesto (see above), plus you can view the photos from this book and a whole bunch of others from our Grand Canyon trip.

www.YukonandBean.com/grand-canyon-slideshow

THE MAKE SOME ROOM MANIFESTO

your brain is **NOT** for remembering.

IT IS EASIER TO KEEP UP | *two minutes now*
than to catch up. | saves hours later.

GETTING ORGANIZED is work; **STAYING ORGANIZED** is habit.

take the time. get quiet. feel into it. immerse yourself.

be discerning about where you spend your energy (reading, doing, watching, eating).

BE BOLD. BE BRAVE. | *laugh.*
TAKE ACTION. | *often and*
even if you're scared shitless while doing it. | *loudly.*

Reclaim your nights and weekends. | **BUSY IS A BULLSHIT WORD.** stop saying it. choose to say something real.

#UNPLUG | *keep only the useful, beautiful, and joyful.*

we cannot know it all, read it all, keep it all, do it all, have it all, or be it all. and that's actually a good thing.

KILL YOUR MICROWAVE. | *stop being a mindless consumer* (of information, products, and food). start caring where "it" comes from.
THROW OUT YOUR TV.

clutter is the inability (or unwillingness) to make a decision. **DECIDE.**

PEOPLE FIRST. technology second. | *say the thing that's the hardest to say* from a place of humility and love (you'll never be sorry).

lay in the grass and listen to the secrets it tells you. | **LOVE**
smile with the flowers. hug the trees. | is all there is.

SLOW DOWN. BREATHE. MAKE SOME DAMN ROOM!

NOTES and IDEAS

57983451R00102

Made in the USA
Charleston, SC
28 June 2016